WHY SHOULD I GO TO ROME

WHY SHOULD I GO TO ↴
ROME

THE CITY YOU DEFINITELY NEED TO
VISIT BEFORE YOU TURN 30 (OR 130)

(m)

THIS IS WHY!

It's hard, maybe even impossible, to find a city that compares to Rome when it comes to history, monuments, art, food, and the overall vibe. The beauty of Rome is something else. It hits you the moment you step onto the *sanpietrini*, the small cobblestones that have been part of the city for centuries.

People have been drawn to the seven hills of Rome for thousands of years. Some came to conquer, others to create. Some built temples and churches, others just soaked it all in. And somehow, all that energy still lingers in the air. Whether you're all about ancient empires, obsessed with art, curious about the Vatican, or just counting down the minutes to *aperitivo* – Rome won't disappoint. It's a city that stays with you long after you've left.

Compared to other European capitals, Rome doesn't have to be hard on your wallet. Food and drinks are surprisingly affordable, and the best way to explore is on foot, as every corner has a story. Whatever you do, make sure you give yourself some time to get a little lost. That's when the best bits happen.

So, why not let one of the many roads lead you to Rome? Come for the ruins, the gelato, the sunsets over the Tiber – or simply all of it.

In bocca al lupo – and enjoy *La Città Eterna*.

CONTENTS

NEIGHBOURHOODS 8
PRACTICAL INFO 12

WHEN TO TRAVEL 30
LIFE IN ROME 40

FOOD AND DRINKS 106
GOING OUT 130

GREEN ROME 170
OUTSIDE OF ROME 184

SHOPPING 142

Index 188
Who made this book? 191-192

NEIGHBOURHOODS

Most sites you'll want to visit in Rome can be found **within the Aurelian Walls**, built by Emperor Aurelian in the third century AD. Inside these walls, Rome is divided into various districts, known as *rioni*.

Centro Storico

The *rioni* making up Centro Storico are where *La Grande Bellezza* happens. Here, you'll find Baroque showstoppers such as Piazza Navona, the majestic Pantheon and the Trevi Fountain. With Caravaggio's and Bernini's whichever way you turn, picture-perfect backdrops all around you, and miles of cobbled streets that have seen it all, Rome's historic centre will certainly leave you in awe. Bordering the Centro Storico lies Villa Borghese, Rome's most famous park.

Monti

Rome's oldest neighbourhood, and one of its most beloved, was called *Suburra* in ancient times. Rome's oldest *rione*, right next to the Fori, was the dodgy part of town in Ancient Roman times. That has changed since and Monti, with its central location, has that perfect bohemian feel. It is a good area for (vintage) shopping and offers plenty of great *aperitivo* spots.

Esquilino

Bordering the train station Roma Termini, Esquilino is a bit off the beaten path and offers a more authentic Roman experience. Once considered the new centre of Rome, Piazza Vittorio was historically a bustling hub, surrounded by shops, cafés, and iconic

markets. Today, it retains a lively atmosphere and among Esquilino's gems are some of Rome's most beautiful churches.

Trastevere

Trastevere is one of Rome's most charming and authentic neighbourhoods. This warm and lively district is full of narrow cobbled streets and vibrant piazzas. A must-see is the Basilica di Santa Maria in Trastevere, one of Rome's oldest churches. Piazza San Callisto is the perfect spot for a coffee or *aperitivo*.

Testaccio

Testaccio is often considered the most authentic neighbourhood within the Aurelian walls. Known for its traditional Roman food scene, this area offers a real taste of Roman life. You'll find an ancient mound of broken pottery in the heart of the district.

OUTSIDE THE WALLS

Vatican City & Borgo

Vatican City is steeped in history and spirituality and is home to two of the most iconic landmarks in Rome: St. Peter's Basilica and the Vatican Museums. The Borgo district offers charming streets lined with cafes and shops, perfect for a peaceful stroll.

Prati

Prati is an elegant neighbourhood known for its wide, tree-lined streets and beautiful early 20th-century architecture. It's ideal for shopping, with Via Cola di Rienzo offering a mix of high-end boutiques and local shops. Close to the Vatican, Prati offers a quieter, more refined atmosphere.

Ostiense & Garbatella

Bordering Testaccio, Ostiense is a vibrant, industrial area that has become increasingly popular for its mix of modern culture and history, and ancient art meets industrial architecture in Centrale Montemartini. Garbatella is known for its street art and unique garden city layout.

Trieste

Trieste's picturesque Quartiere Coppedè is a hidden gem with its eccentric, fairytale-like architecture.

San Lorenzo

Just behind Termini Station, San Lorenzo is a lively, edgy neighbourhood known for its bars, street art, and vibrant nightlife. It's a great place to enjoy good food, music, and a youthful atmosphere.

Pigneto

Pigneto is a trendy, up-and-coming neighbourhood, popular for its bohemian vibe. It's a hotspot for creative types and offers a mix of art galleries, indie cafes, and street art.

Flaminio

Flaminio is a quieter district with a strong cultural scene. North of Piazza del Popolo, the area is home to the MAXXI Museum, showcasing contemporary art and architecture.

TRAVEL

Rome is a very walkable city. Its monuments in the city centre are best reached on foot. Not only is it the best way to soak up the atmosphere and enjoy all the beauty that lies between the landmarks, but it is also completely free. As an example, it takes about 45 minutes to walk from the Colosseum to St. Peter's Basilica – assuming you don't stop for photos, gelato, or a spritz. From Villa Borghese, it's a little over an hour's walk to Testaccio. Along the way, you'll pass the Spanish Steps, the Trevi Fountain, and the *Bocca della Verità*. For the love of everything sacred, only cross streets at traffic lights or zebra crossings. That said, be prepared: cars won't stop until you start walking.

Roma Tremini, the main **train** station, is named after the ancient Baths of Diocletian located opposite the station. These baths, the largest in ancient Rome, could accommodate up to 3,000 people simultaneously and now form part of the National Roman Museum. Adjacent to Roma Termini, you'll find one of the city's oldest surviving archaeological features: the Servian Wall, constructed in the 4th century BC.

For train tickets, you can either queue at one of the slow and somewhat confusing ticket machines, or you can just use the *Trenitalia* app. Look for your train number on the large displays in the hall: the platform number is usually shown about 10-15 minutes before departure. Platforms 25-29 are located at the end of platform 24.

The **underground** system has three lines. Line A, the orange line, runs from southeast to northwest and is convenient for visiting the Basilica di San Giovanni in Laterano, the Spanish Steps, and the Vatican Museums. The blue line B connects the northeast to the southwest, with stops near the Basilica of St. Paul outside the walls, the Pyramid of Caius Cestius, the Circus Maximus, and the Colosseum. Lines A and B cross at Termini. Line C is currently under construction but runs from San Giovanni station to areas in the southeast, such as Pigneto, and will eventually extend to Piazza Venezia. Tap & go – using your card to touch in and out – is available on all metro lines (and is being rolled out across other modes of transport).

The San Giovanni underground station is an attraction in its own right. Along the walls by the escalators, you'll find markers indicating the different historical periods and the corresponding ground levels they once occupied. Inside the station, archaeological artifacts discovered during the excavation of the tunnels are on display, offering a glimpse into Rome's layered history.

Rome's **tram** lines mostly run outside the city centre. However, line 8 offers a convenient connection between Stazione Trastevere and Piazza Venezia. Line 3 passes by Porta Maggiore and continues via Santa Croce in Gerusalemme and San Giovanni in Laterano, skirting behind the Colosseum before reaching the Circus Maximus and the Pyramid of Caius Cestius. It also runs near the charming Quartiere Coppedè.

Buses in Rome can be useful but are not always punctual – so there might be a little wait.

You can purchase **tickets** for metros, trams, and buses at any bar with a blue T sign outside. Don't forget to stamp them once on board, as ticket inspectors show no mercy. For the latest information about public transport in Rome and for information about ticket options, check *atac.roma.it*.

In Italy, hailing a cab is not permitted, and throughout Rome you'll find **taxi** ranks marked with orange signs. Fares are calculated using a meter and are usually very reasonable. Download the *Free Now* app if you'd like to book and prepay a taxi.

Scattered across the city, you'll find **e-bikes** and **e-scooters** available to hire via various apps (Dott, Bird, Link, Lime). When you're finished using them, please park them more considerately than others often do. Riding a scooter with two people is strictly prohibited and you can be fined. Be cautious and mindful of the (many) other people in the city centre.

For trips to the seaside, a local train line runs from Roma Termini through Roma Ostiense and Trastevere, reaching Fregene and Santa Marinella. The Metromare metroline connects Ostiense with Ostia for a quicker route to the coast and ATAC Metrebus Roma tickets are valid on this line (see *atac.roma.it*).

TRAVEL

WHERE TO STAY

Rome is not cheap when it comes to hotels and Airbnb options. Prices vary significantly depending on the time of year. Typically, spring and autumn are more expensive, though in recent years, the low season has been limited to just a few weeks. It's advisable to stay relatively centrally as the outer regions of Rome can be challenging to reach by public transport. With a bit of research, and preferably some flexibility, everyone can find a nice spot that fits their budget.

Suite Art Navona

Via Giuseppe Zanardelli, 20, 00186 Centro Storico, suiteartnavona.com

Found near Piazza Navona, Suite Art Navona is located right in the heart of Centro Storico and very close to Prati. The comfortable contemporary rooms offer a nice contrast to their bombastic baroque surroundings.

Casa Santa Sofia

Piazza della Madonna dei Monti, 3, 00184 Centro Storico, casasantasofia.com

Casa Santa Sofia is in the vibrant Monti neighbourhood and offers affordable accommodation. Overlooking Monti's central Piazza della Madonna dei Monti, this hotel features simple, clean rooms. Its location is close to the Colosseum and the Roman Forum, Piazza Venezia, Quirinal Hill, and Trevi Fountain.

Hotel Griffo

Via del Boschetto, 144, 00184 Centro Storico, hotelgrifo.com

This hotel combines old-fashioned charm with modern comfort in Monti. The boutique hotel has a rooftop terrace with stunning views of Rome. Guests appreciate its proximity to iconic landmarks like the Colosseum while enjoying a quiet, cosy retreat.

Domus Vitra

Via Cavour, 275, 00184 Centro Storico, domusvitra.com

A personal favourite, Domus Vitra is a modern boutique hotel with a minimalist yet very comfortable feel. Situated in Monti, between the Colosseum, Imperial Forums, and Piazza Venezia, Domus Vitra is your perfect home away from home, with the friendliest staff you can imagine.

Jo & Joe

Via delle Quattro Fontane, 113, 00184 Monti, joandjoe.com/roma

This trendy hostel brings a youthful vibe to the heart of Rome. With its colourful design and lively communal spaces, it's an ideal spot for socialising and making new friends. There is a mix of shared and private rooms, ensuring there's something for everyone. Regular events and activities keep the energy high, while the location makes sightseeing a breeze.

Rome Hello

Via Torino, 45, 00184 Esquilino, theromehello.com

This is a fun, welcoming hostel with a friendly atmosphere, making it easy to meet fellow travellers. With a mix of dorms and private rooms, it caters to various budgets. The communal spaces are perfect for socialising, and the staff is always ready to share local tips. Plus, its central location means popular sights are just a short walk away.

The Beehive

Via Marghera, 8, 0018 Esquilino, the-beehive.com

This charming hostel blends a touch of home with a vibrant community spirit. Its warm, inviting decor creates a cosy atmosphere. They organise *aperitivo* nights and city walks, and The Beehive is famous for their bagels. The rooms are clean and simple, and the friendly staff is eager to provide insider tips on local attractions and hidden gems.

La Casa di Amy

Via Principe Amedeo, 85, 00185 Esquilino, lacasadiamy.com

La Casa di Amy offers a delightful, intimate experience for travellers seeking a more personal touch. This family-run hostel will and make you feel part of the family. The charming decor and communal areas encourage relaxation as well as conversation. With a great location near public transport options, it's an easy home base for exploring Rome.

Generator Rome

Via Principe Amedeo, 251, 00185 Esquilino, staygenerator.com/hostels/rome

Generator Rome stands out with its urban, eclectic interior design and comfortable rooms. The hostel features a rooftop terrace with stunning city views, perfect for unwinding after a day of exploring. With a mix of dorm rooms and private options, it caters to different preferences and budgets. The on-site bar and restaurant create a lively atmosphere.

Horti 14

Via di San Francesco di Sales, 14, 00165 Trastevere, horti14.com

Hotel Horti 14 combines the rustic charm of Trastevere with a clean, sleek, modern, luxurious interior. If you are looking to stay in an oasis in the city, this hotel really hits the spot. All rooms overlook the botanical gardens, while you still have major sites and monuments at a stone's throw.

Mama Shelter

Via Luigi Rizzo, 20, 00136 Prati, mamashelter.com/roma

Playful and bold, Mama Shelter Rome is a vibrant hotel with a funky decor and youthful spirit. It features a rooftop bar, communal spaces, and lively restaurants, making it perfect for social travellers or anyone who is working while travelling. Located in the vibrant Prati neighbourhood, it's close to the Vatican and well-connected to the city centre with metro A.

GOOD TO KNOW

Non basta una vita

Rome, the eternal city where ancient monuments meet modern life, with layers and layers (and more layers) of history in between. There is simply too much to see. *Non basta una vita*: a lifetime is not enough. Just don't worry about seeing it all. Savour Rome at your own pace, as every corner has a story to tell. Even if your time in Rome is limited, don't rush. But whatever you do, never skip the Pantheon, enjoy the view of the Forum from the Capitoline Hill, and the stunning Bernini sculptures in the Galleria Borghese. Have some artichokes in the Jewish Ghetto, sip on a spritz in Monti, and stroll through Piazza Navona. Rome is beautiful everywhere, and on every corner, you'll find a new church or a charming street. Soak in the beauty and try to relax despite the impossible task ahead. After all, when in Rome ...

Tickets

If you're planning to visit major attractions like the Colosseum, Vatican Museums, or Galleria Borghese, it's essential to book your tickets as early as possible. Tickets for Galleria Borghese are released sixty days in advance on their official website, and the same applies to the Colosseum. Tickets to the Colosseum are issued in your name, and you'll need to show photo ID at the entrance to verify your booking. To avoid any issues, make sure the name on your ticket matches your ID. Buying tickets for the Vatican can be challenging.

Once time slots are released, they are often quickly snapped up by third-party ticket agencies. Unfortunately, you might have no choice but to purchase tickets through a reseller, often at an increased price.

First Sunday of the Month

On the first Sunday of each month, many of Rome's museums and archaeological sites offer free entry, allowing visitors to explore cultural landmarks like the Colosseum, Roman Forum, and Capitoline Museums. However, free entry results in (much) longer queues, so come early and be prepared to wait. Some sites may have restrictions on opening hours or special services, so check ahead to avoid unexpected delays.

Churches

Rome is home to over 900 churches, many of which house stunning masterpieces by artists like Michelangelo, Raphael, Caravaggio, and Bernini. Churches also offer a peaceful refuge and a cool spot in summer but remember to dress appropriately – knees and shoulders must be covered. Many churches in Rome close for lunch, typically between 1.30pm and 3pm. Most church websites aren't regularly updated, but the opening times on Google maps usually are correct.

Coffee!

Since espresso is the default, that's what you'll get when ordering a *caffè*. It is usually cheaper to drink your coffee standing at the bar, and there is definitely some charm in sipping your *caffè* like a local. In summer, try a *caffè freddo* (cold espresso) or *caffè shakerato* (shaken espresso with ice). Don't hesitate to order a cappuccino during *merenda* around 4pm – it's perfectly acceptable here, despite the 'no cappuccinos after breakfast' myth. But beware, ordering a cappuccino right after

lunch or (the horror!) after dinner is definitely frowned upon.

What time?

Timing is key and Romans do not like to eat 'whenever'. Lunch is typically served between 12.30pm and 2pm, after which many restaurants close for a break. They reopen around 7.30pm to start gearing up for dinner, which usually begins no earlier than 8pm. Restaurants that open before 7.30pm are not necessarily the most authentic.

Gelato

Eating or drinking around Trevi Fountain is prohibited. Sitting on the Spanish Steps is not allowed either. So make sure to take your gelato elsewhere. Speaking of which, avoid brightly coloured ice creams, as those are often artificial. Real *gelato artigianale* has natural colours; banana is a creamy white, and pistachio

has a subtle, greyish-green hue. Also, quality gelato won't be piled on like a mountain but will have a lid or be level with its container.

Going out

Rome is not a city you would visit specifically for its nightlife, but you can find bars and clubs that won't disappoint. The club scene is mainly located outside the city centre. Before diving into Rome's nightlife, it is essential to go out for dinner first. You'll see groups of friends catching up over a plate of *spaghetti al carbonara* before hitting the clubs, instead of gobbling up some greasy fast food after. Clubs only really start to come alive (well) after midnight. At some venues and at certain times, you might have to queue for a table, but that's just part of the experience – and nobody seems to mind.

Safety

I have personally never felt unsafe in Rome – except, perhaps when cycling through Roman traffic on those cobbled streets. This is probably because usually people are out and about until very late at night, especially in the city centre. That said, like in any major city, there are a few things to watch out for – particularly pickpockets. Be extra mindful of your bag, pockets, and surroundings on crowded buses, on the metro, and near major tourist attractions. The usual tourist scams also crop up in Rome. And as for those charming watercolour paintings, you might see artists 'finishing' right before your eyes ... many of them aren't quite as artisanal as they appear. You'll likely spot the same 'unique' painting for sale several times during your stay in Rome.

ROME IN SPRING

Spring is a wonderful time to visit Rome. The city is stunning, with wisteria, jasmine, and oleander starting to bloom. The weather is generally mild, with sunny days perfect for exploring and cool evenings, ideal for al fresco dining. However, Easter weekend is one of the busiest times of the year.

Rome celebrates its birthday on 21st April, commemorating its legendary founding in 753 BC by Romulus and Remus. The city comes alive with historical reenactments, parades, concerts, and festivals, offering a unique way to connect with its ancient history.

During springtime, locals and visitors savour seasonal delights like *carciofi alla Romana* (Roman-style artichokes), or my personal favourite, *puntarelle* (a type of chicory). It is also the perfect time to enjoy Rome's parks, such as Villa Borghese, the Orange Garden, the Municipal rose garden, and the Botanical gardens.

By late April and well into May, the Spanish Steps become even more of a highlight with literally hundreds of blooming azaleas. This is all thanks to Rome's municipal gardening team. They have long been renowned for their expertise in floriculture, tending to a diverse range of plants to enhance the city's green spaces. Based at the historic San Sisto monastery, they cultivate blooms for public display. And since 1952, the iconic azaleas have become a defining feature of Rome's springtime scenery.

ROME IN SUMMER

Summer in Rome can be scorching — think sweaty tourists and melting asphalt. The businesspeople in suits in Centro Storico seem immune to the heat, which only adds to the discomfort — but with some smart planning, you can make the most of it. Take things slow, wear sunscreen, and stay hydrated. You can refill your water bottle at the many *nasoni* (public fountains named after their nose-shaped taps) scattered across the city, offering crisp, fresh, spring water for free.

The 29th of June marks the Feast of San Pietro e San Paolo. The city's patron saints Peter and Paul are celebrated with a solemn mass at St. Peter's Basilica led by the Pope and fireworks over Castel Sant'Angelo lighting up the sky over the River Tiber. The summer months also bring a host of festivals, like open-air cinema screenings and the Lungotevere Festival, with stalls, music, and food along the river.

In August, many Italians leave for their holidays, culminating in Ferragosto on 15th August. While tourist-heavy areas remain busy, quieter residential neighbourhoods offer a welcome respite. Early mornings and late evenings are best for sightseeing to avoid the heat. Or you could cool off with a day trip to the beach, just an hour away by train or car. However, it's important to come prepared. In Santa Marinella, for example, there is hardly any *spiaggia libera* (free beach) left; especially in August or during weekends, come early or reserve a sunbed (and a parasol!) beforehand at one of the *stabilimenti* or hotels renting out sunbeds for the day.

ROME IN AUTUMN

October is widely considered the best month to visit Rome, with warm afternoons and cooler evenings. The tradition of Ottobrata Romana dates back to ancient Roman Bacchanal feasts which gradually became harvest celebrations. Historically tied to grape harvests and communal feasts, they evolved during the 18th and 19th centuries into leisurely countryside outings filled with food, wine, music, and dancing. Though the tradition in its original form has faded, its spirit lives on in Rome's vibrant outdoor culture, with locals and visitors alike embracing al fresco dining, festivals, and events that echo the Ottobrata's celebratory essence. Chestnuts, mushrooms, truffles, and fennel are in abundance.

The Castelli Romani are a perfect day trip during this The Castelli Romani are a perfect day trip during this time of year, since it's the season of the *sagra* — the feasts celebrating the specific crop or food that is associated with a particular town.

In autumn, the *Tramonto Romano* (yes, the sunset needs a nickname) lights up the sky with golden hues, adding to the city's magical charm. Late autumn, particularly late November and early December, brings the mesmerising sight of starlings, whose aerial displays at sunset transform the sky into a living work of art. So find a fancy rooftop bar, bundle up and enjoy the pink sky magically lighting up the Baroque buildings around you. The rooftop season is not over!

ROME IN WINTER

Winter in Rome is magical, especially during the Christmas season, which officially begins on 8th December with the Feast of the Immacolata Concezione. This day is dedicated to honouring the Virgin Mary and her immaculate conception. Piazza di Spagna becomes a focal point as the column of the Immacolata is adorned with flowers.

Throughout the city, churches showcase intricate Nativity scenes steeped in tradition. Piazza Navona hosts a festive Christmas market, where you can find everything from holiday treats to handcrafted gifts. The city sparkles with lights, creating a festive atmosphere despite the cooler temperatures.

Rome's grand Christmas tree traditionally stands proudly on Piazza Venezia. During the reconstruction of Piazza Venezia it can be found on Piazza del Popolo. Beneath Bernini's colonnades, you can admire an exhibition of a hundred additional Nativity displays each year, some of which are quite elaborate.

The first Sunday after Christmas marks the day of the Bambolo Gesù in Santa Maria in Aracoeli. This medieval statue of baby Jesus has been venerated for centuries, believed to possess miraculous powers. On this day, the church holds special masses and prayers to honour the statue and seek its blessings.

As the holidays wind down, the celebration of Epiphany on 6th January, marked by the arrival of La Befana (a witch-like figure flying past in the night, bringing gifts to good children and lumps of coal to the naughty), adds a final festive touch.

HISTORY

Rome is often compared to a *lasagna* — layers upon layers of history forming the city we admire today.

Romulus and Remus

Of the seven hills of Rome, Palatine Hill is the oldest inhabited hill, with people living there as early as the 10th century BC. Legend has it that this is where the she-wolf brought Romulus and Remus, and where Romulus founded Rome on 21st April 753 BC. During the Roman Republic, Palatine Hill was a wealthy district. Augustus built his palace, and subsequent emperors continued to reside in this area. Nero relocated after a fire and built the Golden House (Domus Aurea). This historical hill is filled with fascinating tales and is a must-visit.

Give them bread and circuses

The Colosseum was built by the emperors of the Flavian house who named it the Flavian Amphitheatre to wipe out the legacy of the infamous emperor Nero, but it was the colossal statue of Nero that gave the Colosseum its name. The massive arena hosted gladiator battles and wild animal shows with executions as the intermission act. After the fall of the Roman Empire, the Colosseum lost its original function and took on different roles — it became a fortress, housed small factories, and was even used as a quarry: Colosseum travertine was used to build Palazzo Farnese, Palazzo Senatori, and Palazzo Barberini. Buy tickets online as early as possible. Tickets are personalised, and you'll need photo ID. With a ticket, you can enter the Roman Forum and Palatine Hill on the same day.

Piazza del Colosseo, 1, 00184 Monti, colosseo.it

From Roman Gods to Saints and Popes

Inaugurated in 126 AD, the Pantheon has seen it all. Built initially by Marcus Agrippa in 27-25 BC, it was reconstructed by Emperor Hadrian after a fire damaged the original structure. The massive columns on the façade were transported from Egypt. The interior features a dome with an 8.2-meter-wide oculus that lets the light in, creating a mesmerising effect. The building is a perfect circle, symbolising the unity of heaven and earth. For centuries, the Pantheon was a temple for the gods but was converted into a church by Pope Boniface IV in 609 AD. Officially named the Basilica di Santa Maria ad Martyres, it holds the tombs of important figures like Raphael and the kings of Italy. Every year at Pentecost, rose petals are scattered through the oculus, symbolising the descent of the Holy Spirit, a tradition dating back centuries. An unmissable event for those who are willing to start queuing at 5am.

Fall of the Empire

Depending on how you look at it, the Roman Empire fell more than once. There was the shift to Christianity as state religion in 313 AD (not very Roman), the Sack of Rome by the Visigoths in 410, and then the final fall of the Western Roman Empire in 476. Each moment marked a transformation rather than an absolute end: Rome adapted, reinvented itself, and continued to shape the world in new ways. The Popes took over the emperor's throne, also using the title Pontifex Maximus.

Seers on the Vatican Hill

The Vatican Hill is steeped in history and legend, with various theories surrounding its origins. Some believe that the name Vatican may derive from *vaticinia*, referring to prophets or seers, while others suggest it could have been the site of an Etruscan settlement called Vatica. On the Vatican Hill, the Circus of Nero is infamous as the location where St. Peter was crucified in the 1st century. In the 4th century, the first St. Peter's Basilica was built over his grave, marking the beginning of the Vatican as a centre of Christianity.

Basilica di San Pietro

Construction of the impressive St. Peter's Basilica was initiated by Pope Julius II in the 16th century and was built around and over the old 4th-century structure. The interior of the enormous building is adorned with mosaics, including a copy of Raphael's *Transfiguration* in the left aisle. The statues in the central nave vary in height, with those below standing at 5 meters and those above towering at 7 meters. The basilica's design incorporates elements from the temple of Solomon, with the proportions of the Sistine Chapel mirroring those of the ancient temple, which was plundered and repurposed by the Romans. The iconic dome was designed by Michelangelo.

Piazza San Pietro, Vatican City, basilicasanpietro.va

Via dei Coronari

During the Renaissance, Via dei Coronari became a vibrant street known for its religious artefacts and the procession of pilgrims heading to St. Peter's Basilica. The picturesque street, located in the historic centre of Rome, features charming medieval buildings and Baroque façades. Its name refers to the rosaries once sold by vendors along the route. By the 17th century, the street had transformed into a bustling hub for artists and nobility, influenced by the nearby Piazza Navona and its Baroque landmarks.

Piazza Navona

The site of the former stadium of Domitian had become a dusty town square when the Pamphilijs entered the scene. The Baroque grandeur of Piazza Navona was, as many Roman monuments are, a family affair. When Pope Innocentius X was elected cardinal, his savvy sister-in-law made sure to buy the houses next to the family home to make space for the new palazzo Pamphilij. This palace connected internally to the family church of Sant'Agnese in Agone, designed (partly) by Borromini. Its proximity to Bernini's Fontana dei Quattro Fiumi symbolises the battle between these Baroque titans, whose paths often crossed.

Until the high embankment walls along the Tiber were built, the river would regularly flow over. Piazza Navona, among others, would be submerged. At the corner of Via di Pasquino, you can see a marker indicating the water levels reached during floods like these. More markers can be found at Arco dei Banchi, and Piazza della Minerva, among others.

Spanish?

Known as 'Spanish' in every language except Italian, the Scalinata di Trinità dei Monti was completed in 1725, connecting Piazza di Spagna to the Trinità dei Monti church on top of the hill. They were designed to enhance the area around the church, which was located on an important axis of Roman Catholic pilgrimage as laid out by Pope Sixtus V. The stairs were part of a broader effort to develop Rome's urban space in the early 18th century as

mapped by Giambattista Nolli in 1748. Nolli's map highlights the changing cityscape, showing the integration of churches, squares, and narrow streets into a cohesive urban plan, with the Spanish Steps playing a significant role in linking important landmarks and finishing Sixtus V's final axis.

Unification of Italy

The unification of Italy in the 19th century reshaped Rome's identity, culminating in its designation as the capital in 1871. Key battles unfolded on Gianicolo Hill, where Garibaldi and his volunteers fiercely defended the city against French and papal forces in 1849, laying the groundwork for a unified nation.

Garibaldi

Gianicolo Hill (Janiculum) is a historic site with stunning views of the city, but it is most famously associated with the Italian unification. In 1849, during the Republic of Rome, Giuseppe Garibaldi led a defence against French troops who were sent to suppress the new republic and restore the power of the Pope. Garibaldi positioned his forces on Gianicolo Hill, strategically using the high ground to hold off the attackers. One of the hill's most notable landmarks is the Cannon of Gianicolo. In 1847, Pope Pius IX was fed up with clocks that weren't synchronised and bell towers that all chimed at different times – a daily cannon shot at noon would indicate the correct time, which it still does.

Capital of Italy

To underscore the fact that, after centuries as the city of popes, Rome was now the capital of a unified Italy, a subtle statement wouldn't do. The Vittoriano monument, also housing the Altare della Patria with the grave of the unknown soldier, was completed in 1935 to honour Victor Emmanuel II, the first king.

To mark the fact that Rome was now the capital of Italy and no longer belonged to the Pope, size did matter. For its construction, historical *palazzi*, a tower, and a church had to make way. Many Romans are not fond of it; they find it ugly, referring to it as 'the typewriter' and 'the wedding cake'. When the monument was nearly finished, key members of the construction team had lunch in the horse's belly.

From ancient landfills to urbanisation

Rione Testaccio is a historically rich neighbourhood, named after the ancient Monte Testaccio, a large mound of broken pottery – *testae* – dating back to the Roman Empire. The area developed in the 19th century around the former slaughterhouse, Mattatoio, which operated until the 1970s. Testaccio has since become known for its food markets, modern art spaces (housed in 19th-century buildings on the slaughterhouse site), and lively atmosphere. The neighbourhood borders Ostiense, separated by the Aurelian Wall, where you'll find the Pyramid of Caius Cestius, a striking monument dating back to Rome's republican era when Egypt was 'trending', even though the Egyptian pyramids were as ancient to the Romans as the Colosseum is to us.

Industrial past

The Gazometro (gasometer) is a striking industrial landmark in the Ostiense district. Built in the early 20th century, it was part of the city's gas supply infrastructure. The towering structure, once used for storing gas, now stands as a symbol of Rome's industrial past. In recent years, the area around the Gazometro has become a hub for art and culture, with contemporary spaces, music venues, and restaurants.

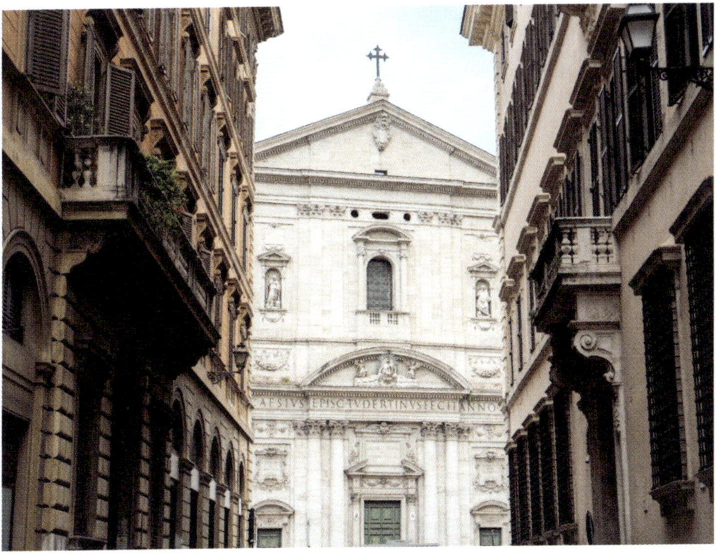
AESIVS EPISC TVDERTINVS FECIT ANNO

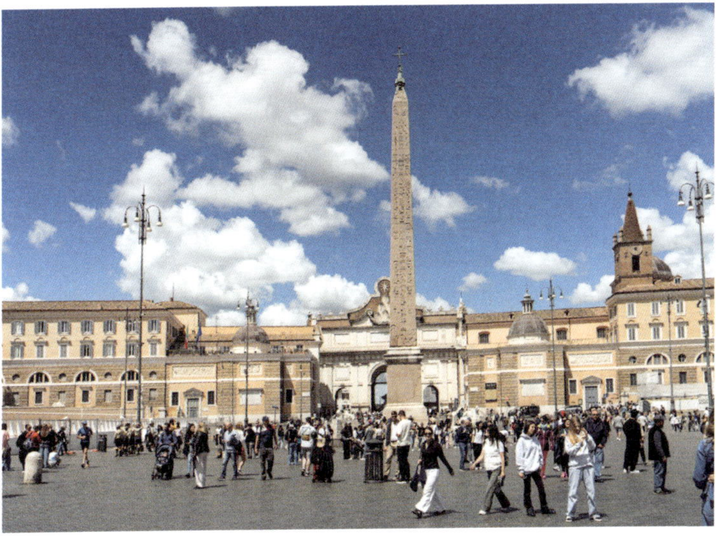

SIGHTSEEING

The Roman Forum, once the centre of political, social, and religious life in ancient Rome, is one of the most important archaeological sites in the city. From Via dei Fori Imperiali, you'll have a beautiful view of the forum. Inside the Santi Cosma e Damiano church, you can get a good sense of the various ground levels from different periods in Rome. The best view over the forum is from behind the Vittoriano Monument (Via di San Pietro in Carcere), and from there you'll feel like you can almost touch the Arch of Septimius Severus. Another great spot is across the Piazza del Campidoglio, the bend of Via del Campidoglio, right behind the Temple of Saturn and the Temple of Vespasian and Titus.

Piazza del Campidoglio

Piazza del Campidoglio, 00186 Centro Storico

This square is the result of a successful collaboration between Pope Alessandro V Farnese and Michelangelo (other examples of joint efforts are the Dome of Saint Peter's Basilica and the Last Judgement in the Sistine Chapel). Piazza del Campidoglio was designed to showcase Rome's recovery and grandeur after the devastation caused by the 1527 Sack of Rome. After the troops of Charles V left Rome in ruins, the emperor visited the city, and the Pope wanted to demonstrate that Rome had not only survived but had emerged stronger. The square, located on Capitoline Hill, the smallest of Rome's seven hills, had to be designed to look as grand as possible to reflect this sense of revival. Michelangelo's design incorporates a blend of Renaissance and ancient Roman elements. The trapezoidal shape of the piazza was one of his key innovations, making it appear more spacious, with the small statues on the roofs of the buildings contributing to that effect.

Piazza Mattei

Piazza Mattei, 00186
Centro Storico

Located in the heart of Rome, in the Ghetto Ebraico, Piazza Mattei is home to the charming Fontana delle Tartarughe. This Renaissance fountain, adorned with bronze turtles attributed to Bernini, is surrounded by quiet streets and historic buildings. A captivating legend claims it was built overnight by a nobleman to impress his future father-in-law. The duke reportedly commissioned the fountain to restore his family's honour after his fiancée's father called off the engagement, doubting the Mattei family's wealth and influence. The sudden appearance of the fountain was intended to showcase their power and ingenuity, ultimately winning back the father-of-the-bride's approval. After impressing with this grand gesture, he had the window bricked up so that no one else could enjoy the same view. In reality, the *Fontana delle Tartarughe* was designed by Giacomo Della Porta in 1581 and sculpted by

Chiesa del Gesù & Sant'Ignazio di Loyola

Piazza del Gesù, 00186 Centro Storico

Taddeo Landini, featuring elegant bronze figures and marble basins. The turtles, which give the fountain its current name, were added in the 1650s, likely by Bernini, during restoration works.

Rome is home to over 900 churches, each contributing to the city's architectural and artistic heritage. Among them, Chiesa del Gesù, built in the 16th century, features Giovanni Battista Gaulli's *Triumph of the Name of Jesus*, a masterpiece of Baroque ceiling frescoes. Nearby, Chiesa di Sant'Ignazio di Loyola impresses with Andrea Pozzo's trompe-l'œil effects, including the famous painted dome illusion. Both churches exemplify the innovation and artistry of Rome's religious architecture.

Santa Maria della Pace & San Luigi dei Francesci

Arco della Pace, 5, 00186 Centro Storico; Piazza di S. Luigi de' Francesi, 00186 Centro Storico

Santa Maria della Pace houses Raphael's exquisite fresco of the *Sibyls*, showcasing his mastery in combining classical themes and Renaissance techniques. Caravaggio also left a trail of masterpieces in Rome. In the church of San Luigi dei Francesi, the last chapel on the left is adorned with his first big commission in Rome: three paintings about the life and death of Saint Matthew. Two of his other important works can be admired in Santa Maria del Popolo.

Santa Prassede

*Via di Santa Prassede,
9/a, 00184 Esquilino*

One of Rome's oldest churches, Santa Prassede is remarkable for its use of *spolia*, recycled Roman architectural elements. It also houses some incredible relics, including a segment of the pillar on which Jesus was flogged, brought back from Jerusalem by Helena, the mother of Emperor Constantine. On her pilgrimage, she also collected soil, which lies underneath Santa Croce in Gerusalemme.

Trevi Fountain

*Piazza di Trevi,
00187 Centro Storico*

No trip to Rome is complete without a visit to the Trevi Fountain. It was completed in 1762, designed by Nicola Salvi and finished by Giuseppe Pannini, marking the final work in the series of *Grande Mostre* commissioned by Baroque popes to enhance the city's architectural beauty. The fountain's dramatic design, featuring the god Oceanus in a chariot pulled by horses, is set against the backdrop of Palazzo Poli. Throwing a coin into its waters (with your right hand over your left shoulder) is said to ensure your return to Rome, throwing in two coins will ensure you'll fall in love with a Roman, and if you can spare three, you will get married.

Piazza del Popolo

*Piazza del Popolo,
00187 Centro Storico*

The Porta Flaminio, connecting Piazza del Popolo and Piazza Flaminio, has been the main access point for all visitors from the north since ancient Roman times. After an enslaved servant assassinated Emperor Nero at the site, he was said to have haunted the area for centuries. According to legend, the Santa Maria del Popolo stands on the site of his tomb. The impressive obelisk in the middle of the square was already shipped from Egypt by Emperor Augustus in the 1st century and was placed here in the 16th century as a marker during the urban renovations of Sixtus V. Bernini gave the gate a makeover in the 17th century for the re-entry of Christina of Sweden. City architect Giuseppe Valadier, also responsible, among other things, for Villa Torlonia, gave the square its current grandeur.

Quartiere Coppedè

Piazza Mincio, 00198 Trieste

Quartiere Coppedè in the Trieste district of Rome was designed in the early 20th century by Gino Coppedè. It was constructed at a transformative period for the city, as Rome shifted from being the Pope's capital to the capital of a unified Italy. This shift led to significant urban changes, including the development of new neighbourhoods. For the design of this area, Coppedè got carte blanche and took full advantage, blending Romanesque, medieval, Art Nouveau, and other styles into a fairytale-like neighbourhood with whimsical charm. During their visit to Rome, The Beatles famously dove into Quartiere Coppedè's showstopping *Fontana delle Rane* – the frog fountain, which was inspired by the *Fontana delle Tartarughe*.

SIGHTSEEING

MUSEUMS

Capitoline Museums

Piazza del Campidoglio 1, 00186 Centro Storico, museicapitolini.org

A true gem and usually not busy. The Capitoline Museums are housed in extraordinary Renaissance *palazzi* and packed with exceptional art. Located on Capitoline Hill, it was the world's first public museum, and it has an exquisite collection of ancient Roman sculptures, including *Lupa Capitolina*, the dying Gaul, and the remaining parts of the colossal statue of Constantine.

Mercati di Traiano

Via IV Novembre 94, 00187 Centro Storico, mercatiditraiano.it

The Museum of the Markets of Trajan is a time capsule of ancient Rome, blending history with incredible views. Built in the 2nd century AD, this multi-level complex was filled with shops and administrative spaces, making it one of the world's first 'shopping malls'. The museum displays treasures from Roman history and offers sweeping vistas of the Roman Forum.

Palazzo Colonna

Via della Pilotta, 17, 00187 Centro Storico, galleriacolonna.it

The Colonna family is one of Rome's oldest nobilities and still is influential in the city and beyond. They have lived in the impressive Palazzo Colonna for centuries and added different wings to it over time. The gallery, open to the public on select days, showcases a rich collection of art, including works by Guido Reni, Carracci, and Veronese. Explore its halls filled with paintings and antique sculptures, reflecting the family's patronage of the arts as well as family paintings, statues, and photos. The palace's gardens are unexpectedly lush. The cannonball on the steps of the gallery has been there ever since the French fired it from Janiculum Hill in 1849, causing surprisingly little damage.

Galleria Doria Pamphilj

Via del Corso, 305, 00186 Centro Storico, doriapamphilj.it/roma

Located in the stunning family residence Palazzo Doria Pamphilj, Galleria Doria Pamphilj has been open to the public since the 18th century. Its collection includes masterpieces by Caravaggio, Titian, and Raphael, and the interior is adorned with opulent furnishings and intricate frescoes, offering a glimpse into the luxurious life of one of Rome's most prestigious families. The audio tour is narrated by Prince Jonathan Doria Pamhilij himself.

↓ CAPOTILINE MUSEUMS

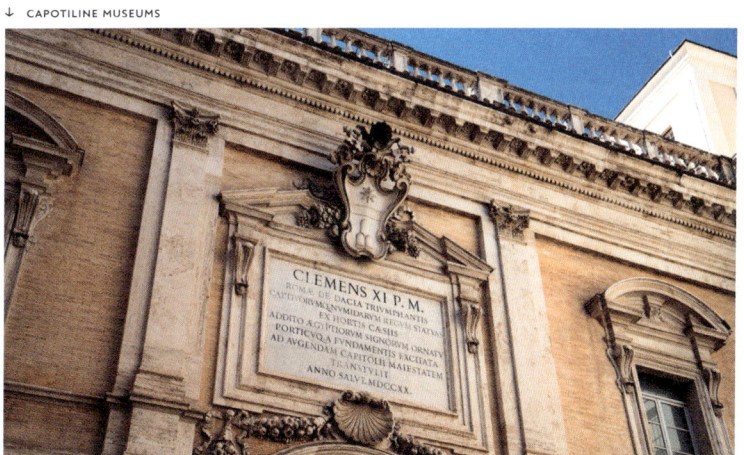

Chiostro del Bramante

Arco della Pace, 5, 00186 Centro Storico, chiostrodelbramante.it

Named after its architect, Chiostro del Bramante is a Renaissance cloister that now hosts contemporary art exhibitions, blending the historical with the contemporary. A quick coffee from the bar overlooking the *cortile* also gives you an opportunity to admire Bramante's Renaissance-precision. In his pursuit of the ideal proportions, he appears to have hidden the corner pilasters within the walls, leaving just a sliver of the capital exposed to maintain visual harmony.

Galleria Spada

Piazza Capo di Ferro, 13, 00186 Centro Storico, galleriaspada.beniculturali.it

Housed in a Baroque palace in the heart of Rome, Galleria Spada showcases an art collection with works by prominent artists like Caravaggio, Guido Reni, and Salvator Rosa. It is also known for the remarkable optical illusion created by Francesco Borromini. His gallery appears to be much longer than it is, showcasing the genius of Baroque architectural innovation. The small gallery offers an intimate experience – if you're lucky, you might find yourself alone in its beautiful halls.

Museo della Forma Urbis

Viale di Parco del Celio, 20, 00184 Celio, sovraintendenzaroma.it

The Museo della Forma Urbis is dedicated to the cartographic history of Rome. By 'the' cartographic history, we mean the Forma Urbis Romae, an enormous marble map of ancient Rome, which offers a detailed view of the city in its prime. This museum provides a fascinating insight into Rome's urban evolution and is an essential stop for anyone interested in the city's history.

Galleria Borghese

Piazzale Scipione Borghese, 5, 00197 Villa Borghese, galleriaborghese.beniculturali.it

Within the picturesque Villa Borghese gardens, you'll find one of the most beautiful museums in Rome. Galleria Borghese houses the largest Caravaggio collection in the city, and the museum also holds Bernini's earliest masterpieces, including *Apollo and Daphne* and *The Rape of Proserpina*, showcasing his extraordinary ability to bring marble to life. Proserpina's rear alone is worth the visit. Among the highlights is Canova's sculpture of Pauline Bonaparte, depicted as *Venus Victrix*. It is rumoured that when her husband, Prince Camillo Borghese, expressed distress over her posing nude, Pauline casually retorted 'Don't worry, I wasn't cold.'

Palazzo Massimo alle Terme

Largo di Villa Peretti, 2, 00185 Esquilino, museunazionaleromani.beniculturali.it

Part of the Museo Nazionale Romano and home to an important collection of ancient art. Palazzo Massimo's exhibitions include classical sculptures, frescoes, mosaics, and artefacts from Roman life, most of which have been excavated during the construction of Stazione Roma Termini. Highlights include the well-preserved frescoes from the Villa of Livia, the famous *Boxer at Rest* sculpture, and a remarkable collection of ancient Roman portraits.

Galleria Corsini

Via della Lungara, 10, 00165 Trastevere, barberinicorsini.org

Palazzo Corsini, a Baroque palace along the banks of the River Tiber, houses Galleria Corsini. The gallery boasts an impressive collection of paintings from the 15th to the 18th century, including works by Caravaggio, Rubens, and Velázquez. The collection is displayed in a series of elegant rooms, with opulent frescoes and richly decorated interiors. The gallery provides a glimpse into the tastes and artistic patronage of the Corsinis, one of Rome's most prominent noble families.

Villa Farnesina

Via della Lungara, 230, 00165 Trastevere, villafarnesina.it

Villa Farnesina is a Renaissance villa in a dreamy garden in Trastevere. It was built by wealthy banker Agostino Chigi and changed to its current name when the Farnese family who owned a palazzo right across the Tiber bought it as their holiday home. Chigi's villa was decorated by famous artists such as Raphael, Sebastiano del Piombo, and Baldassarre Peruzzi. Its frescoes, particularly the *Galatea* and those of *Cupid* and *Psyche* (all Raphael), are Renaissance masterpieces. The Habsburg soldiers who occupied the villa during the 1527 Sack of Rome left some interesting graffiti on the second-floor walls.

Vatican Museums

Viale Vaticano, 00165 Vatican City, museivaticani.va

The excavation of the Laocoön group in 1506 marked the beginning of the Vatican Museums. Since then, galleries, halls, and miles of rooms filled with art have been added. Highlights of the Vatican Museums include the *Augustus* of Prima Porta, the octagonal hall with, alongside the Laocoön Group, some gems by Canova, the Galleria delle Carte Geographiche, the Raphael Rooms, and the Sistine Chapel. Tickets for the Vatican Museums are hard to come by through the official website, and are often sold through third parties. Although the museums get very crowded, art and history lovers really should allow a good few hours to visit the museums. The architecture, the beautiful chapels and impressive galleries, as well as the enormous collection of antique sculptures and paintings by the greatest

↓ VATICAN MUSEUMS

masters, are absolutely stunning and the experience remains totally unique.

Castel Sant'Angelo

Lungotevere Castello, 50, 00193 Borgo, beniculturali.it

Originally built as a mausoleum for Emperor Hadrian, Castel Sant'Angelo has served as a fortress, papal residence, and prison. Today, it is a museum that showcases the rich history of the castle, including its transformation over the centuries. The museum's exhibits range from ancient Roman artefacts to Renaissance weaponry and papal collections. A visit to the castle will take you down ramparts, along the route once taken by ancient burial processions, all the way up to enjoy unique near-360-degree panoramic views of the city.

Centrale Montemartini

Via Ostiense, 106, 00154 Ostiense, centralemontemartini.org

Part of the Capitoline collection is presented in former power plant Centrale Montemartini, offering an exciting contrast of ancient sculptures against industrial machinery. Originally conceived as a temporary exhibition space for surplus pieces from the Capitoline Museums, the unexpected harmony between classical art and 19th-century technology captivated visitors. This success led to its establishment as a permanent exhibition as a satellite location of the Capitoline Museums, creating one of Rome's most unique cultural spaces.

MAXXI

Via Guido Reni, 4a, 00196 Flaminio, maxxi.art

The National Museum of 21st Century Arts (MAXXI) is Rome's leading institution for contemporary art and architecture. Designed by celebrated architect Zaha Hadid, the museum is known for its futuristic design, featuring sweeping curves and dynamic spaces. MAXXI houses a vast collection of modern and contemporary works. It is a hub for innovation and creativity, hosting regular exhibitions and events that explore the latest trends in art, design, and architecture. The museum's engaging environment and diverse collection make it an essential destination for lovers of contemporary culture.

↓ VATICAN MUSEUMS

STREET ART

Portrait of an old man

Via Urbana/Piazza degli Zingari, Monti

Borondo's powerful portrait on one of Monti's many picturesque corners captures the weathered face of an elderly man, conveying deep emotion and the passage of time. The portrait speaks of resilience and memory, and the stories etched in the lines of old faces as well as places.

I still remember how it was before

Via Roma Libera/ Via Emilio Morosini, Trastevere

In Trastevere, British street artist My Dog Sighs has created a stunning mural featuring 540 eyes, each with an iconic part of the Roman skyline reflected in them. This mural is about nostalgia and memories of the past, mirroring the historical cityscape within personal reflections.

Lupa

Via Galvani, Testaccio

Without the she-wolf, would Rome even exist? In Testaccio, often said to be the last true Roman neighbourhood within the walls, Belgian street artist ROA has paid tribute to Rome's legendary origins in a spectacular way. ROA's powerful, dynamic depiction brings this symbol to life, celebrating the animal that suckled Romulus and Remus, the twin brothers who, according to legend, founded Rome. It captures the spirit of the city's enduring legend.

Fronte del Porto

Via del Porto Fluviale, Ostiense

BLU uses his unique style to explore themes of control, freedom, and human impact on the environment. His artworks in Ostiense have become an iconic part of the city's street art scene. In his massive mural *Fronte del Porto* on Via del Porto, BLU used the architectural elements of the building as a guide for an array of striking and bizarre imagery, including human figures intertwined with animals, machinery, and bananas. BLU's work on this building prevented its demolition: a win-win.

Hunting Pollution

Via del Porto Fluviale/Via del Gazometro, Ostiense

Iena Cruz's *Hunting Pollution* is strikingly beautiful. The mural — depicting a heron holding prey in its beak and tentacles rising from the water behind its feet — was created using special paint that breaks down pollutants. Blending art with sustainability, it not only offers a visual spectacle, but it also contributes to the purification of the urban environment.

Nessuno

Via del Porto Fluviale, Ostiense

A bit further down Via del Porto Fluviale, Axel Void's mural *Nessuno* depicts a solitary figure — a woman viewed from behind. Despite this viewpoint, it is unmistakably evident that she is melancholically gazing into the distance. The title, *Nessuno* ('nobody' in Italian), amplifies this sense of loneliness and anonymity, making the artwork especially resonant within its urban setting.

Muri Sciuri/ Big City Life

Via Tor Marancia, 63, Garbatella, bigcitylife.it

Garbatella is known for its vibrant street art largely due to the Big City Life project which originated to bring colour, light and life into this neighbourhood. The result is an open-air street art museum featuring eighteen magnificent murals.

Tutti in Bici

Via dei Peligni, San Lorenzo

In San Lorenzo, Simone Ferrarini, in collaboration with Collettivo FX, created *Tutti in Bici*, a mural that celebrates cycling as both a sustainable mode of transport and a symbol of freedom in urban life. Against a vibrant blue background, a little girl is riding a bike, accompanied by many more cyclists within her shadow.

Il suono del tempo

Via del Mandrione, 3, Pigneto

With the mural *Il suono del tempo* ('Sound of time'), Luca Zamoc blends classical heritage and modern urban life. Featuring the ancient Belvedere Torso, it situates the figure between the railway lines and a Roman aqueduct, creating an evocative contrast between Rome's ancient history and its industrial present. The mural symbolises the enduring presence of the past in the city's modern landscape, while also inviting reflection on the passage of time and the continuous transformation of the urban environment.

STREET ART

CINEMA

These days, most films can be watched in the original language in Italy, and dubbed films have become less prominent. To make sure you are able to follow the dialogue of the flick you've chosen, look for the abbreviation *V.O., V.O.S.* or *V.O.S.I.* in the listing. If neither label is present, a film is likely dubbed (*doppiato*).

Cinema Barberini

Piazza Barberini, 26, 00187 Centro Storico, cinemabarberini.it

Located near the iconic Piazza Barberini, this cinema offers a mix of Italian and international films, including some screenings in English. Most films are shown in their original language with subtitles in Italian. It is known for its excellent selection of both mainstream and indie films.

La Casa del Cinema

Largo Marcello Mastroianni, 1, 00197 Villa Borghese, casadelcinema.it

This cultural venue in the beautiful Villa Borghese Park is dedicated to classic cinema. They host retrospectives, film festivals, and screenings of timeless films in a comfortable and inviting setting. Films are typically shown in their original language with Italian subtitles. It's the perfect spot for film enthusiasts looking to dive into cinematic history and enjoy a peaceful day in one of Rome's most scenic locations.

Cinema dei Piccoli

Largo Marcello Mastroianni 14, 00197 Villa Borghese, cinemadeipiccoli.com

Cinema dei Piccoli is a tiny historic cinema in the Villa Borghese park. Housed in a small green wooden structure, it originally opened in the 1930s and still has a nostalgic feel. By day, children's films are shown, and in the evenings, independent and international films are screened, often in their original language.

Cinema Troisi

Via Girolamo Induno, 1, 00153 Trastevere, cinematroisi.it

Cinema Troisi is a lively cultural hub in the heart of Trastevere. This modern cinema offers a 300-seat theatre and a range of additional facilities, including a study space, bar, and an intimate outside space. With a focus on young audiences, it hosts a variety of films, from international blockbusters to independent cinema, alongside cultural events. Most films are shown in their original language with Italian subtitles.

Cinema Nuovo Sacher

Largo Ascianghi 1, 00153 Trastevere, sacherfilm.eu

Cinema Nuovo Sacher is a small, independent movie theatre in Rome, founded by local filmmaker Nanni Moretti. It is known for its cosy red velvet seats and quiet, laid-back vibe that draws in a loyal crowd. You won't find any blockbusters at Nuovo Sacher: its focus is on European arthouse films and emerging directors. It is a great spot for thoughtful, well-made films outside the mainstream options.

FESTIVALS

Cortili Aperti

In May, Cortili Aperti ('Open Courtyards') offers a unique chance to explore the hidden courtyards of Rome's historic buildings. Several private courtyards open their doors to the public, showcasing beautiful gardens, art installations, and live performances.

comune.roma.it

Opera Terme di Caracalla

At the ancient Roman Baths of Caracalla, an awe-inspiring archaeological site, Opera Terme di Caracalla takes place from June to August. The open-air Teatro dell'Opera hosts spectacular opera performances, including famous productions like *Aida* – a magical experience.

operaroma.it

Lungotevere Festival

The Lungotevere Festival is an open-air event held from late June until the end of August along the River Tiber, offering a mix of music, theatre, film viewings, bars, terraces, art, and karaoke.

insta @lungoiltevere.official

Villa Celimontana Jazz Festival

The Villa Celimontana Jazz Festival is a must-attend event for jazz lovers. Held in the beautiful Villa Celimontana Park from June to September, it features performances by top international and Italian jazz musicians.

villagecelimontana.it

Videocittà

Held in July on the site of the Gazometro in Ostiense, Videocittà is an innovative audiovisual festival that showcases a wide range of moving images, including screenings, performances, workshops, and immersive installations.

videocitta.com

Il Cinema in Piazza

This outdoor film festival takes place on various piazzas across Rome in June and July. During Il Cinema in Piazza, a range of films, from classic Italian cinema to contemporary international films, is screened.

ilcinemainpiazza.it

Festa dei Noantri

From mid-July, this historic festival is celebrated in dedication to the Virgin Mary of Donnalbina. With origins in the 16th century, Festa dei Noantri features religious processions, music, and local food, reflecting the vibrant community traditions of Trastevere.

turismoroma.it

Villa Medici Film Festival

The French Academy in Rome, Villa Medici, organises September film screenings in its beautiful gardens: a must for film lovers and a unique opportunity to admire the beautiful villa.

villamedici.it

Ottobrata Romana

This festival, with roots dating back to Ancient Rome, celebrates the region's agricultural heritage in October. Traditionally celebrated in the fields (*prati*) around the city and celebrating the harvest, Rome now has many Ottobrata celebrations, including a popular one in Monti.

ottobratamonticiana.com

THINGS TO DO

Via Appia Antica

Via Appia Antica, one of the oldest roads in Rome, is a walk or bumpy bike ride through history. Lined with ancient ruins, aqueducts, and catacombs, each step seems to take you back in time a little bit further. If you have a day to spare (and have buns of steel), a bike ride from the *via* to Lago Albano would be a nice outing.

Roma Sotterranea

Most of Ancient Rome lies unexcavated beneath the modern city. Exploring underground with a guided tour past ancient crypts, aqueducts, and long-forgotten temples is as educational as it is thrilling. Roma Sotterranea's team consists of geologists, architects, engineers, and archaeologists organising and guiding tours below the eternal city.

sotterraneidiroma.it

Cooking Class at Roscioli

Cooking classes are offered far and wide, but when in Rome it makes sense to join one of the city's oldest culinary families to prepare your own lunch. Learn to prepare traditional Roman dishes such as handmade pasta, meatballs, and *tiramisù*, paired with a wine tasting. Classes are held from Wednesdays to Sundays at noon.

Via del Conservatorio, 58, 00186 Centro Storico, rimessaroscioli.com

Domus Aurea

Although part of the Parco Archeologico del Colosseo, the guided tour of the Golden House of Nero is often overlooked by tourists. A dive into the splendour of Nero's Domus Aurea will leave you in awe of the ancient frescoes, architecture,

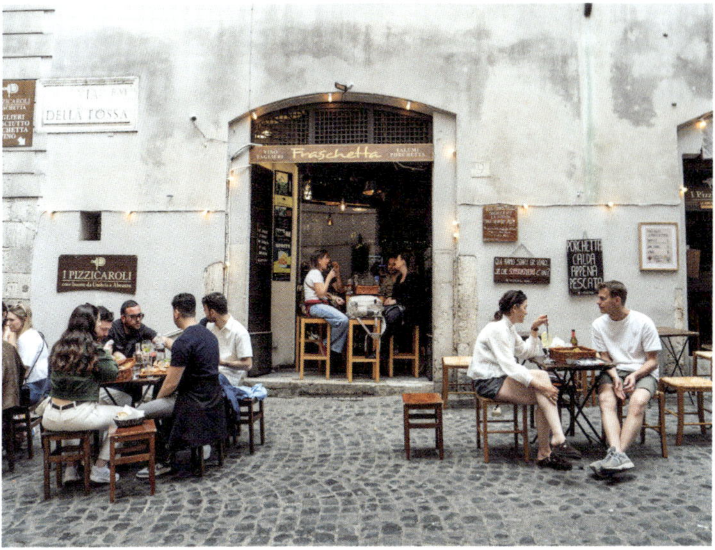
DELLA FOSSA
Fraschetta
I PIZZICAROLI
PORCHETTA
CALDA
APPENA
PESCATA

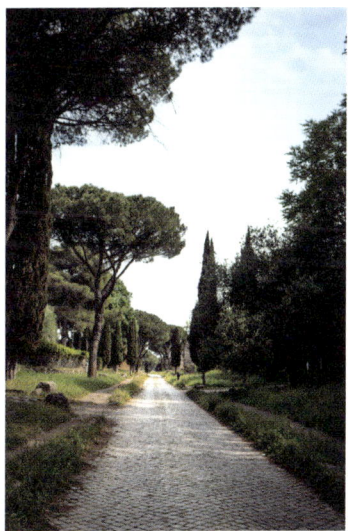

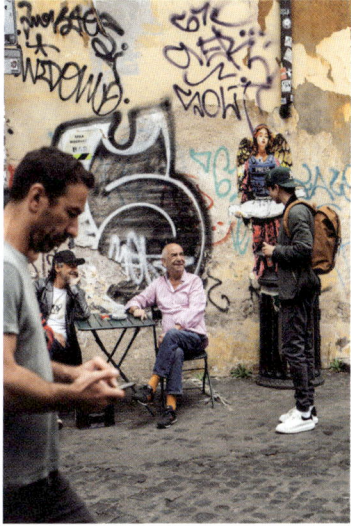

and grandeur of the complex that was torn down and buried to make room for the Colosseum. Tickets for tours of the Domus Aurea are sold separately.

Viale della Domus Aurea, 00184 Monti, colosseo.it

Mosaic Workshop

At Studio Cassio, near the Colosseum, you can try your hand at the ancient art of mosaic making. Learn traditional techniques and create your own masterpiece. Open to all skill levels, this workshop is a wonderful way to engage with Roman craftsmanship.

Via Urbana, 98, 00184 Monti, studiocassio.com

Boat Rental

For a cheesy but charming outdoor activity, rent one of the small boats at the tiny lake in the Villa Borghese Gardens. Circle around the picturesque Temple of Aesculapius, and soak in the tranquillity of this emerald refuge right in the heart of the city.

Viale dell'Aranciera, 00197 Villa Borghese

The Sistine Chapel Extra Time Tour

The Sistine Chapel is truly breathtaking. However, navigating the crowds can make you feel like Moses before parting the Red Sea. For a more relaxed experience, the extra costs of the Extra Time Tour are worth it. This guided tour takes you through the museums and the Sistine Chapel just after the last regular visitors. Its highlight is the semi-exclusive visit to the Sistine Chapel. Afterwards, enjoy an *aperitivo* in Bramante's Cortile della Pigna.

Vatican City, museivaticani.va

Frascati Wine Tour

Escape the city and explore the countryside with Old Frascati Food & Wine Tours. Just a short train ride away, Frascati offers charming family-run wineries and bakeries. Learn to make pizza and pasta from scratch, taste local Frascati wines, and enjoy beautiful vineyard views.

Via Frascati Colonna, 25, 00044 Frascati, oldfrascati.com

FAMOUS PEOPLE

Alessandro Borghi

Born in Rome, Alessandro Borghi's role in *Suburra*, in which he portrayed Aureliano Adami, the manically ambitious son of an Ostia mafia boss, established him as a key figure in modern Italian cinema.

Audrey Hepburn

Without Audrey Hepburn, there might not even be a queue of people waiting to stick their hand into *Bocca della Verità*. The influence of the film *Roman Holiday* on post-war tourism in Rome was just that big. Admiring great Roman monuments as a runaway princess, Hepburn herself loved the city and lived in it for many years.

Beatrice Cenci

Beatrice Cenci is a tragic figure in Roman history, whose life and death have captured the imagination of many. Born into an aristocratic family in the late 16th century, her life took a dark turn when she was involved in the murder of her abusive father. Beatrice's trial and execution took place in 1599. It is said that every year since, on 10th September, her ghost appears on Ponte Sant'Angelo, carrying her own bloody, severed head.

Damiano David

Risen to fame after winning the Eurovision Song Contest in 2021 and conquering the international music scene in rock band Måneskin and as a solo artist, Damiano David is as Roman as they come. In fact, all band members are true Romans, and Måneskin was formed in the city — making their famous Circo Massimo performance a full-circle moment.

Ennio Morricone

Born in Rome, Ennio Morricone was a legendary Italian composer. He was famous for his scores for 'Spaghetti Westerns', including *The Good, the Bad and the Ugly*. Morricone composed over 500 film scores throughout his career and is celebrated in his hometown with the Auditorium Parco della Musica Ennio Morricone.

Federico Fellini

Federico Fellini was an Italian film director, famous for his surreal and imaginative style, particularly in films like *La Dolce Vita* and *8½*. Fellini's works are often semi-autobiographical, drawing from fantasy as well as reality. Although Rome plays a central role in his films, the master did not like to shoot on the streets of the city but preferred filming in the Cinecittà studios.

Gaius Julius Caesar

Gaius Julius Caesar was a Roman general and statesman, famously known for his role in the expansion of the Roman Empire and the pivotal part he played in the fall of the Roman Republic. He was famously assassinated by his close allies on the Ides of March in 44 BC. Caesar's relationship to Rome is profound, as he reshaped its political landscape a bit too much for the senators' liking.

Gian Lorenzo Bernini

Gian Lorenzo Bernini was *the* sculptor and architect of the Roman Baroque era. Bernini's influence on Rome is immense and it is virtually impossible to visit Rome without falling for his masterpieces. Bernini worked for many Popes, but

it was pope Urban VIII who, still known as Cardinal Maffeo Barberini at the time, held a mirror so Bernini could use his own face as an example for his *David*.

Mister OK

When making New Year's resolutions, it's best to dive straight in, like Mister OK does. Every New Year's Day, Mister OK dives from Ponte Cavour into the River Tiber, getting his nickname from the *I'm OK* gesture he makes to the crowd watching him from the bridge.

Pastaqueen

Born and raised in Rome, Nadia Caterina Munno, better known as Pastaqueen, is an Instagram celebrity and food blogger, known for her fun and accessible approach to cooking Italian dishes. She gained fame with her traditional Italian recipes, sense of humour and *La Dolce Vita* sensuality.

Pope Stephen VI

Pope Stephen VI is infamous for his role in the Cadaver Synod, in which he exhumed the body of his predecessor Pope Formosus and put it on trial. Stephen had Pope Formosus' corpse dressed in papal robes and propped up to face charges.

Pope Julius II

Pope Julius II, known as 'The Warrior Pope', participated in military campaigns to defend and take back lost territory of the Papal States. He installed the Swiss Guard. Julius was also famous for his patronage of the arts. He commissioned Michelangelo to paint the Sistine Chapel's ceiling, Bramante to build the 'new' St. Peter's and Raphael to decorate his private apartments at Vatican.

Tony Servillo

Born near Naples but having lived in Rome for many years, Tony Servillo must be included in this list if only for his role as Jep Gambardella in Paulo Sorrentino's Oscar-winning *La Grande Bellezza*.

FILMS & SERIES IN AND ABOUT ROME

Cinecittà Studios, or 'Hollywood on the Tiber', is one of the most famous film studios in Italy, having been home to iconic films like *Ben-Hur*, *La Dolce Vita*, and *Gangs of New York*. Visitors can explore sets, exhibitions, and learn about both Italian and international cinema, making it a must-see destination for lovers of cinematic magic.

Ladri di Biciclette (The Bicycle Thief, 1948)

This Vittorio De Sica classic is a landmark in Italian neorealism. Set in the streets of Rome, it tells the story of a poor man searching for his stolen bicycle, capturing the struggles of post-war Rome's working class. Di Sica always shot on location and never worked with professional actors, giving his films an authentic quality.

Roman Holiday (1953)

In *Roman Holiday*, Audrey Hepburn and Gregory Peck tell the story of a runaway princess and her day in Rome to life. The film showcases iconic landmarks like the Spanish Steps, the Colosseum, and *Bocca della Verità*.

La Dolce Vita (1960)

Federico Fellini's *La Dolce Vita* depicts the life of a tabloid journalist amidst Rome's elite. The famous Trevi Fountain scene, starring Anita Ekberg, is a defining moment in both the film and the history of Rome in cinema.

Ieri, Oggi, Domani (Yesterday, Today, and Tomorrow, 1963)

This comedic anthology, directed by Vittorio De Sica, features three segments about Italian life. One is set in Rome, with Sophia Loren and Marcello Mastroianni exploring love, culture, and the complexities of relationships.

Gladiator (2000)

Gladiator, directed by Ridley Scott, is an epic historical film set in ancient Rome. Russell Crowe stars as Maximus, a general seeking revenge against Emperor Commodus. The film's spectacular use of CGI to recreate ancient Rome's grandeur makes it one of the most iconic depictions of the Roman Empire in contemporary cinema.

Rome (2005-2007)

HBO's *Rome* delves into the transition from the Roman Republic to the Roman Empire. Filmed in the city, the series vividly reconstructs ancient Roman life, portraying the rise of Julius Caesar and the fall of Pompey.

La Grande Bellezza (The Great Beauty, 2013)

La Grande Bellezza, directed by Paolo Sorrentino, is a modern exploration of Rome's decadence through the eyes of a jaded journalist. The film's stunning visuals highlight Rome's timeless beauty alongside its contemporary indulgence, winning the Oscar for Best Foreign Language Film.

The Young Pope (2016)

Paulo Sorrentino's surreal, over-the-top and intriguing TV series *The Young Pope*, starring

Jude Law as Pope Pius XIII, was filmed in Rome, and every shot is beautifully composed. It explores the (fictional) intersection of power and faith within the Vatican, with the city's historic sites providing a dramatic backdrop.

Suburra: Blood on Rome (2015)

This Italian crime drama uncovers Rome's criminal underworld, where politics, crime, and the church intersect. *Suburra* became a global hit after its release on Netflix in 2017. With all the layers of Rome as an extra character and a beautiful backdrop, the series offers a cinematically beautiful but gritty view of the dark side of the city.

The Two Popes (2019)

The Two Popes explores the candid relationship between Pope Benedict XVI and the future Pope Francis. Shot in Rome, the film highlights key Vatican locations, adding depth to its portrayal of the religious and political world.

Ripley (2022)

The TV series *Ripley* (2022), based on Patricia Highsmith's *The Talented Mr. Ripley*, includes scenes filmed in Rome. The story follows Tom Ripley, a young man who deceives his way into high society, with the Eternal City's glamorous locations serving as the perfect backdrop.

Nuovo Olimpo (2023)

This romantic drama was filmed entirely in Rome. The story follows two men from Rome, who fall in love, lose each other, and then reconnect years later. As their relationship develops, they wander past the Fori, Trastevere, and the streets near Piazza Navona, making the eternal beauty of Rome a third character in the film.

Conclave (2024)

Conclave is a political thriller set within the Vatican during a papal election. The film, based on Peter Straughan's 2016 novel, explores the drama and intrigue surrounding the selection of a new pope. It attracted renewed interest following the death of Pope Francis in April 2025 and was re-released in Italian cinemas.

BOOKS IN & ABOUT ROME

Rome Stories – Various authors

Rome has inspired countless writers over the years. Some of the most interesting, moving and beautiful stories have been collected in *Rome Stories*. A pleasant read on your own Roman holiday as it contains multiple short stories. Some of them old (Goethe, Stendhal), some of them very old (Livy), some of them more recent (Pier Paolo Pasolini), all of them offering a unique take on the city.

Eternal City – Ferdinand Addis

A must-read for history nerds or anyone who wants to devour all layers of Rome, *Eternal City* weaves together 3,000 years of Rome's history – from Romulus to *La Dolce Vita*.

SPQR – Mary Beard

Mary Beard's *SPQR: A History of Ancient Rome* is a comprehensive exploration of the Roman Republic's rise and fall. Beard delves into the lives of ordinary citizens, highlighting the social dynamics, politics, and events that shaped the Roman world. Not a casual read, but a must if you truly want to understand all about Rome's ancient past.

Angels and Demons – Dan Brown

This novel blends historical intrigue with fast-paced action, offering a unique (if not entirely factual) view of Rome through the lens of mystery and suspense. While the plot of *Angels and Demons* keeps you on the edge of your seat, don't expect it to be a history lesson. Much of it is, shall we say, creatively fiction-

alised, with a generous helping of historical 'nonsense' sprinkled in for dramatic effect.

Italian Journey – Goethe

Johann Wolfgang von Goethe's *Italian Journey* is a travelogue detailing his time in Italy during the late 18th century. The book chronicles Goethe's exploration of Rome and other Italian cities, offering deep reflections on art, culture, and philosophy. His observations capture the essence of Rome during a time of great change, and his writing remains an essential resource for understanding the city's influence on European thought.

Rome – Robert Hughes

If you're looking for an overview of the Eternal City's different eras, Robert Hughes offers a rich, engaging narrative of the city's history in *Rome*. From its founding to the present day, Hughes explores Rome's transformations, key figures, and pivotal moments masterfully. The book blends art, history, and architecture to create a captivating portrait of a city that has profoundly shaped Western civilization – although, as with most historical narratives, a certain level of romanticism is involved.

Michelangelo and the Pope's Ceiling – Ross King

Michelangelo and the Pope's Ceiling tells the unbelievable story behind the creation of the Sistine Chapel's iconic vault. Focusing on Michelangelo's struggles and triumphs during its painting, King explores the tensions between the artist and Pope Julius II, the challenges of the project, and the profound impact the work had on art and religion. The book paints a vivid picture of the Renaissance, offering insights into one of Rome's greatest masterpieces.

The Families Who Made Rome – Anthony Majanlahti

Borghese, Pamphilij, Colonna, Corsini, Barbernini ... the names of *The Families Who Made Rome* are to be found all over the city and this book dives into these influential families, detailing how they shaped Rome. With the perfect blend of history and *juice*, this book combines historical storytelling with itineraries that follow each family's trail.

24 Hours in Ancient Rome – Philip Matyszak

Historian Philip Matyszak invites readers to step back in time to experience a day in the life of a Roman citizen. The book provides an immersive account of what daily life was like in Ancient Rome, from breakfast to bedtime, each hour through the eyes of a different Roman, covering everything from politics and religion to leisure and food. It's a detailed, fascinating snapshot of Roman life at the height of its empire.

The Ragazzi (The Street Kids) – Pier Paolo Pasolini

This novel captures the youthful energy and drama of East Rome's gritty streets of the 1950s. Set against the backdrop of the city's most famous locations, *The Ragazzi* centres around a group of teenagers navigating life in post-war Rome. With its mix of youthful rebellion, friendship, and romance, the story offers an intimate look at the city from a younger generation's perspective.

FUN FACTS

Renaissance it girl

Raphael's *Sybils* adorn the walls of the Chigi Chapel in Santa Maria della Pace, exuding heavenly beauty and representing fate intertwined with divine knowledge. One of the Sybils was modelled after Imperia, Renaissance 'it girl', courtesan, and lover of Agostino Chigi, the wealthy banker who commissioned the work.
Arco della Pace, 5, 00186 Centro Storico

Intense legacy

Caravaggio's time in Rome, though brief (fourteen years), was marked by a deluge of masterpieces that still captivate art lovers today. His revolutionary use of *chiaroscuro* (light and shadow) and his ability to capture raw human emotion set him apart. While he may have been a genius with a paintbrush, he was well known for his fiery temper and run-ins with the law.

Historic Paddling Pool

Before aircon, the summer heat even became unbearable to the wealthy residents of Piazza Navona. To cool off, they once blocked the drains of Bernini's *Fountain of the Four Rivers* with stones, flooding the square to turn it into a makeshift paddling pool. A whimsical way to escape the heat, although probably not what Bernini had in mind.

Inside the horse's belly

When the enormous monument to King Vittorio Emmanuele II was nearing completion, the builders had an unusual lunch: inside the belly of the horse

statue! This quirky moment in history showcases the scale and ambition behind this iconic monument.

Rome's Underdog Hero

Born into humble circumstances, Cola di Rienzo rose to power in 14th-century Rome with big ideas, calling himself the 'Tribune of the People'. Inspired by ancient Rome, he fought against the corrupt elite but quickly fell from grace. His dramatic rise and fall became a symbol of Rome's struggle for civic freedom, though history didn't look too kindly on his ambitious plans.

German Graffiti

In 1527, the Sack of Rome occurred, when troops of Charles V stormed the city, looting and causing chaos. Habsburg soldiers, who participated, left behind a trail of 'graffiti', some of which can still be found on buildings like the Palazzo dei Conservatori. This chaotic moment in history led to the creation of Michelangelo's Campidoglio, designed to restore Rome's dignity.

Third Capital

Did you know that Rome wasn't the first capital of Italy? It was actually the third, following Turin and Florence. This little-known fact reminds us that Rome's status as the heart of Italy came much later, despite its central role in history.

Trevi Fountain's Charity

Every day, about 3,000 euros is collected from the Trevi Fountain and donated to Catholic charities. This practice has been ongoing for decades, making the famous fountain not only a place for wishes to be made but also a source of charity for those in need.

The Sabine Women

According to legend, Rome was founded in 753 BC by Romulus and Remus, twin brothers raised by a she-wolf after being abandoned as infants. The founding myth takes a dark turn when Romulus kills Remus. Having populated his city with thugs and other obscure figures, Romulus and his Roman friends invited their neighbours, the Sabines, over for a feast and abducted their women. When the Sabines got back on their feet and returned a year later, the women – in what might be described as the first case of Stockholm syndrome – actually preferred to stay.

What Lies Beneath

Believe it or not, only about ten per cent of ancient Rome has been excavated. There's still much of the Eternal City waiting to be uncovered, and who knows what hidden gems lie beneath the *sanpietrini*, just waiting to tell their stories!

PHOTO SPOTS

Giardinetto del Monte Oppio

For a breathtaking panoramic view of the Colosseum, with few to no aspiring influencers, head to the Giardinetto del Monte Oppio. This garden, located on Oppian Hill, provides a stunning spot to capture one of Rome's most iconic landmarks. It's the perfect place to get that dramatic Colosseum shot, framed with lush greenery, and offers a serene contrast to the crowds below.

Piazza del Popolo

Piazza del Popolo is a grand, spacious square, perfect for capturing the classic Roman urban landscape. From the centre of the square, you'll get a wide-angle view of the twin churches of Santa Maria in Montesanto and Santa Maria dei Miracoli, looking into the three streets that make up the *tridente*. And the ancient Egyptian obelisk is a bonus. Climb the steps to the Pincio Gardens for an elevated view of the piazza and the skyline stretching towards the Vatican.

Ponte Umberto I

If you're looking for a classic Rome shot, Ponte Umberto I offers one of the best views of the Castel Sant'Angelo and St. Peter's Dome. The bridge itself is a beautiful setting for photos, with the river in the foreground and the majes-

tic landmarks of Rome rising in the background. It's a perfect spot to capture the essence of Rome's blend of ancient and modern architecture.

Via del Campidoglio

*Via del Campidoglio
00186 Centro Storico*

The bend in Via del Campidoglio gives you a picture-perfect view of the majestic ruins of the ancient temples and government buildings on the Forum Romanum. Walk to Piazza Cafferelli, on the opposite end of Piazza del Campidoglio, and you can enjoy an impressive view of the massive white marble structure of the Vittoriano monument.

Palazzo Braschi (Museo di Roma)

Piazza di S. Pantaleo, 10, 00186 Centro Storico, museodiroma.it

From the window on the second floor of Palazzo Braschi, you can enjoy a view over Piazza Navona, one of the most beautiful Roman squares. Capture the stunning Baroque architecture, including Bernini's *Fountain of the Four Rivers*, and the vibrant atmosphere of the square below. It's an excellent spot to take in both the history and the lively energy of the area.

Pantheon

Piazza della Rotonda, 00186 Centro Storico, direzionemuseiroma. cultura.gov.it/pantheon

One of the most clichéd yet unique photo opportunities in Rome is looking up at the Pantheon's famous dome. The view from inside the Pantheon, especially when you stand directly beneath the oculus, provides a striking shot that captures the ancient architecture and the light streaming in. It's a perspective that shows the true grandeur of this ancient wonder.

Santa Maria Maggiore

Piazza di Santa Maria Maggiore, 00100 Monti

For a captivating photograph of Santa Maria Maggiore, walk down Via Panisperna. The view from this street gives a perfect angle of the basilica's dome, framed by the surrounding buildings. It's an underrated photo spot that showcases the majesty of one of Rome's four papal basilicas with an urban backdrop.

Trajan's Column

Via dei Fori Imperiali, 00187 Monti

The iconic Trajan's Column, commemorating Emperor Trajan's victory in the Dacian Wars, is a perfect subject for photos. The best spot to capture the column in all its grandeur is from the bend of Via Quattro Novembre, where you can get a clear shot of the column surrounded by the hustle and bustle of modern-day Rome, juxtaposing the ancient with the contemporary.

Via Margutta

Via Margutta, 00187 Monti

A picturesque, quiet street tucked away from the crowds, Via Margutta is known for its charming art galleries and quaint atmosphere. It's a beautiful location to capture the classic Roman vibe, with its narrow, cobbled streets, ivy-clad buildings, and traditional shutters. The street has been immortalised by famous artists and filmmakers, and it offers a peaceful retreat for a more intimate, classic shot of Rome.

Trastevere

Piazza di Santa Maria Maggiore, 00100 Monti

Trastevere's narrow, winding streets are some of the most photogenic in Rome. Capture the charm of the district by wandering through its alleyways, where the traditional Roman architecture, colourful buildings, and cobbled streets create beautiful photo opportunities.

BREAKFAST

A typical breakfast in Rome consists of a cappuccino or *caffè* accompanied by something sweet like a *cornetto* or a *maritozzo*, a typical Roman breakfast pastry filled with very thick whipped cream. Its name, 'husband' stems from the custom to hide engagement rings in the cream for marriage proposals. At most cafés, you pay at the till first, then take your receipt to the counter to order. Enjoy your breakfast like the Romans do, standing at the bar (*al banco* is usually cheaper), having a little chat, leave some change for the barista, and whatever you do, don't lick the foam from your spoon ...

Tazzo d'Oro & Sant'Eustacchio

The debate over the best coffee in Centro Storico seems as eternal as the city and we are not here to end it. Finding bad coffee in Rome is nearly impossible anyway. However, if you find yourself near the Pantheon, the perfect pick-me-up is served at either Tazzo d'Oro or Sant'Eustacchio il caffè.

Via degli Orfani, 84, 00186 Centro Storico, tazzadorocoffeeshop.com
Piazza di S. Eustachio, 82, 00186 Centro Storico, caffesanteustachio.com

Bar Farnese

If you're near Campo de' Fiori, stop by Bar Farnese, where barista Angelo has been serving coffee – and charm – for over sixty years. It's a timeless Roman experience in one of the city's most atmospheric locations.

Via Dei Baullari, 20, 00186 Centro Storico

Mercato Plebiscito

Mercato Plebiscito is a bar, a restaurant, and a food court.

Grab a cappuccino and a *cornetto* from Plebiscito's bar and enjoy a quiet breakfast in the peaceful courtyard of Palazzo Venezia.

Via del Plebiscito, 104, 00186 Centro Storico, plebiscito.net

Antico caffè Grecco

The oldest bar in Rome was opened in 1760 by a Greek owner, hence the name. You won't find many locals here, but the décor is worth going for. It's not the cheapest option, but the price at the bar is quite reasonable. Plus, having a *caffè* at the same bar where Goethe, Stendhal, Lord Byron, and Liszt once were regulars is worth the rate.

Via dei Condotti, 86, 00187 Centro Storico, anticocaffègreco.eu

La Licata

A true Monti classic. The espresso machine is always running, and while it's always bustling, the atmosphere remains welcoming and unhurried. Whether you sit on their outdoor space (with a view of the Colosseum) or snag a window seat, it's perfect.

Via dei Serpenti, 165, 00184 Monti, barlalicata.it

Forno Conti

A neighbourhood favourite, Forno Conti is a traditional Roman bakery known for its fresh pastries and rustic bread. It's a great spot for a quick breakfast with a quality espresso and a *cornetto* straight from the oven. Locals stop by for their morning fix or to pick up some baked goods to go.

Via Giusti, 18, 00185 Esquilino, fornoconti.co

Casa Manfredi

At Casa Manfredi, you'll find insanely delicious pastries paired with exceptional coffee. This is the kind of place where every bite feels like a little masterpiece – perfect for those who appreciate the art of a great Roman breakfast.

Viale Aventino, 91/93, 00153 San Saba, casamanfredi.it

Pasticceria Linari

For that quintessential neighbourhood feel, a moment to slow down, and a classic Roman coffee experience, Pasticceria Linari in Testaccio is the perfect spot. This charming little bar will satisfy your sweet cravings with its delicious pastries and authentic atmosphere.

Via Nicola Zabaglia, 9, 00153 Testaccio, pasticcerialinari.com

Pasticceria Andreotti dal 1931

A true classic, Andreotti has been serving traditional Roman breakfasts since the 1930s. With its timeless charm and enduring quality, it's the perfect spot to experience a slice of authentic local history with your coffee and *cornetto*.

Via Ostiense, 54 b, 00154 Ostiense, andreottiroma.it

Faro – Caffè Specialty

One of Rome's pioneers in specialty coffee, Faro offers expertly brewed espresso, filter coffee, and alternative brewing methods. With a focus on high-quality beans and precise preparation, it's a must-visit for coffee lovers.

Via Piave, 55, 00187 Salario, farorome.com

LUNCH

Rome doesn't have a brunch tradition, but going out for lunch is a cherished ritual. Especially on Sundays, the *pranzo della domenica* is iconic. Most restaurants mentioned are also great dinner options. Many close between 3pm and 7pm.

Libera Soon

Breakfast bar, lunchroom, aperitivo spot, and home décor shop in one, Libera Soon has an almost un-Roman minimalist, industrial gallery feel. Located on the quietest street around Piazza

Navona, it has a great collection of home goods and is a good stop all day.

Via del Teatro Pace, 41, 00186 Centro Storico, @liberasoon

Maccheroni

Given its location between Piazza Navona and the Pantheon, it's no surprise that Maccheroni attracts tourists. However, the authentic ambience, traditional pasta dishes, and loyal Roman patrons prove it's far from a tourist trap. Inside, you can watch the bustling kitchen, where pots of pasta are constantly on the stove, and plates are moved at lightning speed.

Piazza delle Coppelle, 44, 00186 Centro Storico, ristorantemaccheroni.com

Zia Rosetta

Zia Rosetta headlines Rome's quintessential bun, *rosetta.* If the number of options on the menu dazzles you, opt for three mini buns. If there aren't any available seats, take your lunch to Piazza degli Zingari.

Via Urbana, 54, 00184 Monti, ziarosetta.com

Tiberino

On the Isola Tiberino, overlooking the Piazza San Bartolomeo all'Isola, Tiberino's terrace is one of the best. The food is tasty, the wine delicious, and the sun is probably shining. What's not to like?

Via di Ponte Quattro Capi, 18, 00186 Trastevere, tiberinoroma.it

Borgosteria

Finding a good lunch spot near the Vatican can be a challenge. Borgosteria, however, is the perfect place to recharge and relax after exploring the Vatican Museums. Its vibrant ambience and satisfying dishes make it an oasis amidst the crowds.

Borgo Pio, 161, 00193 Borgo, insta @borgosteria161

Forno Roscioli

The Rosciolis are somewhat legendary in the Roman food scene. Forno Roscioli in Esquilino is famous for its fantastic *pizza rossa* but also offers a *tavola calda* buffet-style lunch. And it is affordable too.

Via Buonarroti, 46/48, 00185 Esquilino, fornoroscioliesquilino.it

200 Gradi

Another great option near the Vatican, especially if you don't want to sit down for lunch, is 200 Gradi. Known for its incredible variety of sandwiches, the only downside is the overwhelming number of tempting choices – perfect for a quick yet delicious bite.

Piazza del Risorgimento, 3, 00192 Prati, duecentogradi.it

La Zanzara

Situated in the Prati district, La Zanzara is an elegant yet casual spot where locals and visitors alike come for everything from an espresso at the bar to a full Roman meal. Its contemporary vibe and versatile menu make it stand out in the area.

Via Crescenzio, 84, 00195 Prati, lazanzararoma.com

Necci dal 1924

Necci's garden is a lush haven in the heart of Pigneto. The perfect place for lunch, *aperitivo*, or dinner for those who have made it to this 'new' part of town. The menu is versatile with lots of healthy options, international dishes, and Roman classics.

Via Fanfulla da Lodi, 68, 00176 Pigneto, necci1924.com

Dar Ciriola

Famous for its sandwiches made with traditional Roman bread, Dar Ciriola offers an authentic taste of Rome in a simple yet satisfying format. Whether filled with cured meats, cheeses, or seasonal vegetables, these sandwiches are the perfect on-the-go treat.

Via Pausania, 2a, 00176 Pigneto, insta @darciriolu.it

STREET FOOD

The Roman street-food scene is about 2,000 years old. As the five-storey-high *insulae* that housed Rome's 'lower classes' didn't have kitchens, people often ate at food stalls. Fires broke out when they did try to cook at home, and the thick greyish wall that is still standing between what is now the Monti district and the Imperial Forums was erected mainly to protect the public space from outbreaks of fire in the Suburra. Today, the street food on offer is as tasty as ever.

Supplizio

Supplì, crispy fried rice balls with tomato and gooey mozzarella (*al telefono*, as the stringy cheese resembles an old-fashioned telephone cord), are a Roman street-food staple. Supplizio is the perfect spot to get them.

Via dei Banchi Vecchi, 143, 00186 Centro Storico, supplizioroma.it

Trapizzino

Another Roman favourite is the *trapizzino*, a cross between a pizza and a sandwich, filled with traditional Roman ingredients. Originating in the quintessential Roman *rione* Testaccio, *trapizzini* have gained popularity beyond Rome, with locations in Milan, Florence, and even New York.

trapizzino.it

Pizza al taglio

Pizza al taglio, pizza by the slice, is served in rectangular pieces cut to your preferred size. You can find this all over Rome, with popular spots including Antico Forno Roscioli, Forno

Campo de' Fiori, Alice – a Roman chain now found throughout Italy – and La Renella. For a gourmet twist, visit Bonci Pizzarium in Prati.

Via della Meloria, 43, 00136 Prati, bonci.it

MARKETS

Large supermarkets are rare in central Rome. Romans prefer to do their daily shopping at local markets. You can grab a classic lunch-on-the-go by grazing your way through one of the many markets.

Mercato Rionale Monti

At this neighbourhood market, some small tables are set up where you can enjoy your *panino* that has just been freshly made exactly as you like it.

Via Baccina, 36, 00184 Monti, fb @mercatomonti

Mercato Testaccio

Mercato Testaccio features a variety of stalls offering fresh produce, meats, cheeses, and baked goods. If you are looking for a takeaway sandwich, Mordi e Vai is the favourite. There are tables and small seated areas where you can sit down to enjoy your food.

Via Aldo Manuzio, 66b, 00153 Testaccio, mercatoditestaccio.it

Mercato Trionfale

A true taste of Rome, Mercato Trionfale is one of Italy's largest markets and one of the most popular in Rome. Over 250 stalls sell an impressive array of goods. From seasonal fruits and vegetables to fresh fish and meats, the stalls are brimming with colourful produce. The friendly vendors are always keen to share their knowledge of the products.

Via Andrea Doria, 41, 00192 Prati, mercatotrionfale.store

Mercato Campagna Amica al Circo Massimo

At the farmers market near Circo Massimo, fresh, seasonal produce comes straight from local farms. The market, only open on weekends, is housed in an interesting industrial building, this is not just a market for functional shopping.

Via di S. Teodoro, 74, 00186 Ripa, mercatocircomassimo.campagnamica.it

SHOPS

Castroni

Castroni, founded in 1932 in Prati, has been a key player in Rome's culinary scene. The store is known for its wide selection of Italian products, from pasta and coffee to spices and fine wines. If you are keen on taking some culinary souvenirs home, stop by.

Via Cola di Rienzo, 196/198, 00192 Prati, castronicoladirienzo.com

Eataly

Eataly Rome is located in in the Ostiense district inside a spacious complex that was once an industrial building. It offers a wide selection of Italian food products, regional specialties, restaurants, and cooking workshops, making it a perfect destination for food lovers looking for authentic Italian ingredients in one spot.

Piazzale 12 Ottobre 1492, 00154 Ostiense, eataly.net

GELATO

There are many *gelaterie* in Rome that hold the unofficial title of 'the best'. But if you run into any gelateria of the chains Fatamorgana, Gelateria La Romana or Gelateria dei Gracchi, you should join the queue. They can be found all over Rome.

gelateriafatamorgana.com
gelateriaromana.com
gelateriadeigracchi.it

Gelateria del Teatro

A special mention must go to Gelateria del Teatro, where all ingredients are fresh and locally sourced – except for the strawberries, which sometimes are shipped in. After all, children craving strawberry ice cream must never be disappointed.

Via dei Coronari, 65/66, 00186 Centro Storico, gelateriadelteatro.it

APERITIVO

Sharing an *aperitivo* is a way of life in Rome. The Italians tend to have a drink before dinner to unwind, and not just on Fridays – but they never overdo it. A decent *aperitivo* is not hard to find, but we suggest a few good options that offer a smooth transition between lunch and dinner.

Camillo dal 1890

Out of all the outdoor seating surrounding Piazza Navona, only Camillo's is loved by the locals. Opened by the current generation's great-grandfather, the bar has recently undergone a renovation. Their *aperitivo* menu is extensive but the view of Bernini's Fontana dei Quattro Fiumi really seals the deal.

Piazza Navona, 79-81, 00186 Centro Storico, camillopiazzanavona.it

La Buvette

Slightly upscale with a NY/Parisian-inspired interior, La Buvette is a lovely spot for an *aperitivo* and really a great place all day. It is located between Piazza del Popolo and the Spanish Steps. The wine list is carefully curated. Drinks don't come cheap, but bites are included.

Via Vittoria, 44/47, 00187 Centro Storico, insta @labuvetteroma

Salotto 42

Aperitivo-wise, it really pays off not to just plop down in front of the Pantheon but to walk down Via dei Pastini and enjoy your spritz overlooking the Temple of Hadrian. Salotto 42 has more than just the regular spritz on the menu, and a unique selection of bites to go with it.

Piazza di Pietra, 42, 00186 Centro Storico, salotto42.superbexperience.com

Civico 4

Located in the heart of Monti, Civico 4 is a low-key spot in the perfect location. Both locals and visitors seem to have a hard time passing by. They have an *aperitivo* menu that includes different bites on individual platters, Roman *pinsa*, and a dinner menu that changes regularly.

Via degli Zingari, 4, 00184, Monti

Tram Depot

Tram Depot, found at the foot of Aventine Hill on the edge of Testaccio, is a charming outdoor bar set in a repurposed tram. With wonderful seating under the trees and exceptionally friendly staff, it's a great spot to enjoy a drink any time of day, although it's closed in winter. Note that there are no toilets.

*Via Marmorata, 13, 00153 Testaccio, insta @tramdepot_*

Bibliobar

Fancy a read (and a view) with your *aperitivo*? Bibliobar is an outdoor bar and library with seating between Castel Sant'Angelo and the Palace of Justice (aka *Palazzaccio*, or 'ugly palace'). It is a perfect spot to unwind after a long day of sightseeing.

Lungotevere Castello, 00193, Borgo

PIZZA

Traditionally, a classic round pizza is seen as a dinner dish. Roman pizza is quite different from the more famous Neapolitan, as it has a thin, crispy base. Great spots for pizza include Ivo a Trastevere and Ai Marmi.

Via di S. Francesco a Ripa, 158, 00153 Trastevere, ivoatrastevere.it
Viale di Trastevere, 53-59, 00153 Trastevere, fb @aimarmi

DINNER

Osteria delle Copelle

This family-run *osteria* serves classic Italian dishes in a setting that has found the perfect balance between elegant and relaxed. Osteria delle Copelle has a great outdoor seating area that is set up as soon as the neighbourhood market on the square closes. It is also a great spot for an *aperitivo*.

Piazza delle Copelle, 54/55/56, 00186 Centro Storico, osteriadellecoppelle.com

Giulio Passami l'Olio

This relaxed, no-frills restaurant offers classic Roman dishes, including a truffle-topped *cacio e pepe*, alongside an impressive wine selection with over a thousand options. The friendly atmosphere makes it ideal for a casual evening with friends.

Via di Monte Giordano, 28, 00186 Centro Storico, giuliopassamilolio.it

Il Marchese

Not even a ten-minute walk from Piazza Navona, Il Marchese is a restaurant and *amaro* bar in one. A bit posh, but with a very welcoming atmosphere and a menu filled with Roman classics.

Via di Ripetta, 162, 00186 Centro Storico, ilmarcheseroma.it

Pianostrada

Pianostrada brings a contemporary edge to Roman dining with its chic décor and innovative menu. The restaurant focuses on fresh, high-quality ingredients, crafting dishes that are as visually stunning as they are delicious. Ideal for food lovers looking for a modern dining experience, it's a standout in Rome's evolving culinary scene.

Via della Luce, 65, 00153 Centro Storico, pianostrada-laboratoriodicucina.it

Ristorante Brocoletti

Ristorante Brocoletti is one of those places that gets everything just right, with the ideal mix of traditional and contemporary. Their menu features classics with a twist, they serve some fabulous wines, and the friendly, welcoming owners and staff really know their trade. Hosting an impressively local crowd for a Monti restaurant, this is the kind of place you'll want to return to again and again.

Via Urbana, 104, 00184 Monti, insta @ristorantebroccoletti

Rocco

This Monti neighbourhood classic has recently started to attract a younger crowd while maintaining their old-school clientele. Located just off the beaten tourist paths, you'll find mostly locals at Rocco. Not too fancy for a weekday but definitely not your average place, and you can't go wrong here.

Via Giovanni Lanza, 93, 00184 Monti, fb @Rocco-Ristorante

La Trattoria de Gli Amici

Gli Amici is more than just a restaurant; it's a social project run by a cooperative supporting individuals with disabilities. This heartwarming trattoria serves authentic Roman food in a friendly, inclusive environment. It offers attentive service and food prepared with love.

Piazza di S. Egidio, 6, 00153 Trastevere, trattoriadegliamici.it

Felice a Testaccio

A Roman institution, Felice a Testaccio is renowned for its iconic *cacio e pepe*. This trattoria, nestled in the heart of Testaccio, combines decades of culinary expertise with a warm, welcoming atmosphere. Their preparation of Roman dishes is simple yet flawless.

Via Mastro Giorgio, 29, 00153 Testaccio, feliceatestaccio.com

Trattoria Da Enzo al 29

Tucked away in Trastevere, Da Enzo al 29 consistently draws crowds for its authentic Roman fare, often with a queue of people waiting before they open. Despite its popularity, it retains the charm of a family-run trattoria.

Via dei Vascellari, 29, 00153 Trastevere, daenzoal29.com

Trattoria Pennestri

In Ostiense, Trattoria Pennestri offers a fresh take on traditional Roman cuisine. Classic dishes are given creative twists, and the extensive wine list includes organic options. With seasonal menus and warm hospitality, it's a perfect spot for a relaxed evening with friends.

Via Giovanni da Empoli, 5, 00154 Ostiense, trattoriapennestri.it

BRING THE PARENTS

Ristorante Piperno

Right in the heart of the Jewish Ghetto, Ristorante Piperno offers a historic setting for traditional Roman dining. Known for its rich history and classic dishes like *carciofi alla giudia* (Jewish-style fried artichokes), the feel of this restaurant is charmingly formal, and the service is all you would expect.

Via Monte dè Cenci, 9, 00186 Centro Storico, ristorantepiperno.it

Pierluigi

Rome's 'elite' and those who want to see and be seen flock to Pierluigi for a night of fine dining. Located on Piazza de' Ricci, which looks like a movie set, this restaurant is renowned for its exquisite seafood and sophisticated ambience. Its service is as impeccable as the white jackets of the servers.

Piazza de' Ricci, 144, 00186 Centro Storico, pierluigi.it

Six Senses Rome

Looking for an upscale dining experience in a chic, contemporary setting? Six Senses Rome delivers just that. With a menu focused on fresh, locally sourced ingredients, this sleek space offers a sophisticated yet comfortable environment for a lavish meal.

Piazza di San Marcello, 00187 Centro Storico, sixsenses.com

Oro Bistrot

One of the latest additions to Rome's rooftop scene, Oro Bistrot looks out over the Forum of Trajan and the Vittoriano. A tad over the top but with a view that will blow you away — like the prices, but then again: the view!

Via di S. Eufemia, 19, 00187 Centro Storico, orobistrot.it

Terrazza Borromini

More than just a place to eat, Terrazza Borromini is about the experience. Located next to the stunning Borromini bell towers of the church of Sant'Agnese in Agone, the views of Piazza Navona are unparalleled. While the prices on the cocktail menu reflect the prime location, the breathtaking panorama makes it worth the splurge.

Via di Santa Maria dell'Anima, 30, 00186 Centro Storico, terrazzaborromini.com

GOING OUT

BEER

Antica Birreria Perroni

Located near the Trevi Fountain, Antica Birreria Peroni has been serving beer since the early 20th century. Inside, nostalgia seems to flow as abundantly as the beer from the tap. Enjoy your beer with a simple, classic dish and admire the antique cityscapes of Rome on display on the panelled walls.

Via di S. Marcello, 19, 00100 Centro Storico, anticabirreriaperoni.it

Ma Che Siete Venuti a Fà

A staple of the Italian craft beer scene since 2001, Ma che siete venuti a fà in Trastevere is known for its expertly curated selection of national and international brews. With sixteen rotating beers on tap, each beer is poured with care to highlight its unique characteristics. They host regular events involving breweries and microbreweries. Casual and as unpretentious as possible, it remains a favourite for both locals and visitors looking for quality craft beers.

Via Benedetta, 25, 00153 Trastevere, football-pub.com

Jungle Juice

Birrificio Jungle Juice is a brewpub, also offering guided tours. The vibe is industrial, and the beer list is equally robust. Offering something for everyone, from craft beers to exotic cocktails, Jungle Juice is a lively space.

Via del Mandrione, 109, 00181 Pigneto, junglejuicebrewing.com

WINE

Il Piccolo

Tucked away on Via del Governo Vecchio, Il Piccolo remains refreshingly authentic despite the surrounding tourist spots. The menu is straightforward, offering around ten reds and ten whites, along with a selection of *salumi*, cheeses, and simple snacks. A favourite among locals, it's an unpretentious spot to relax with a good glass of wine in the heart of Rome.

Via del Governo Vecchio, 74-75, 00186 Centro Storico, insta @enoteca_il_piccolo

Il Goccetto

This charming wine bar has been a popular spot since what feels like forever. Time stood still, but in a good way. Offering a wide variety of wines by the glass, it's a great place to explore the best of Italy's wine regions. At night, customers stand outside with their glasses of Barbera, Montepulciano, or ... the choice is endless.

Via dei Banchi Vecchi, 14, 00186 Centro Storico, insta @thereal_ilgoccetto

Enoteca Buccone

Enoteca Buccone has been a go-to spot for wine lovers since 1969, offering an impressive selection of wines by the glass, including rare and high-quality labels. The racks of wine bottles are stacked to the ceiling, representing all Italian regions, from major wineries to rare and particular wines.

Via di Ripetta, 19/20, 00186 Centro Storico, enotecabuccone.com

Al Vino Al Vino

In a seemingly underwhelming building (the competition from the view of the Colosseum at the end of the street does not help), Al Vino Al Vino is the kind of enoteca where the wine list steals the show, and not necessarily the interior. When it comes to snacks and bites, the *caponata* is a must!

Via dei Serpenti, 19, 00184, Monti

BARS

Tartarughe

Located on Piazza Mattei, one of Rome's most picturesque squares (see page 53 for the fountain's story), this spot is open all day buw especially perfect for a scenic *aperitivo*. The relaxed setting makes it ideal for people-watching while enjoying a spritz or Italian wine.

Piazza Mattei, 7/8, 00186 Centro Storico, tartarughebar.it

Bar San Calisto

Along with the Pantheon, Saint Peter's, and the Colosseum, Bar San Calisto is a true Roman icon. Since the 1960s, they have been serving coffee to the ladies returning from the San Cosimato market, and beer to the men playing cards. At night, Piazza San Calisto turns into an open-air bar, and as the bar prices are just as nostalgic, there's no reason not to get another *spritz*.

Piazza di S. Calisto, 3, 00153 Trastevere, barsancalisto.it

Samovar

If you are looking for a bit more comfort but with the same Trastevere energy, walk across the square to Samovar. This is a vibrant bar with a great cocktail list, the perfect outdoor space for people-watching, and somehow the kind of place where you end up having interesting discussions with complete strangers.

Piazza di S. Calisto, 00153 Trastevere, insta @samovar_trastevere

Freni e Frizioni

One of Rome's most iconic *aperitivo* bars, Freni e Frizioni in Trastevere is always buzzing, blending industrial charm with eclectic décor and attracting a laid-back creative crowd. Known for strong cocktails and a generous vegetarian-friendly *aperitivo* buffet, it's a lively spot near the Tiber, perfect for drinks and people-watching.

Via del Politeama, 4, 00153 Trastevere, freniefrizioni.com

Bar dei Brutti

Bar dei Brutti in San Lorenzo is not for the faint of heart, but if you look past the 'rustic' décor, you'll find a great spot for a laid-back drink in the heart of the neighbourhood.

Via dei Volsci, 71-73, 00185 San Lorenzo, insta @bardeibrutti

QUEER

Coming Out Roma

Coming Out, near the Colosseum, has been a key LGBTQ+ venue since 2001. Open all day, it offers international breakfast options, Roman cuisine, and lively evening events, including drag shows and live DJs. With its welcoming atmosphere, it's a favourite haunt for the LGBTQ+ community and allies alike, offering great drinks in a vibrant space.

Via San Giovanni in Laterano, 8, 00184 Monti, comingout.it

My Bar

Known for its inclusive environment, My Bar in the heart of Rome's LGBTQ+ scene offers a fun, friendly ambience and a wide range of cocktails. It's a great place to socialise, with music filling the air most evenings.

Via di S. Giovanni in Laterano, 12, 00183 Monti, insta @mybar.roma

CLUBS

Check websites or socials for special events, info about advance booking (especially recommended for groups), and dress codes or door policies.

Sharivari

A popular club in the city centre. You can go to Sharivari for an *aperitivo* followed by a dinner buffet, as well as for dancing until the early hours. The music is fairly commercial, and the crowd is young and international. It can be a bit touristy but it's still a fun club with plenty of space to dance.

Via de' Nari, 14, 00186 Centro Storico, sharivari.it

The Sanctuary

The Sanctuary is another popular nightclub. There's often some queuing involved, with those who have connections getting preferential treatment. But once inside, you can enjoy exotic cocktails in a magical setting, surrounded by beautiful people.

Via delle Terme di Traiano, 4A, 00184 Monti, thesanctuaryecoretreat.com

Alcazar Live

Located in the heart of Trastevere, Alcazar Live is a cinema that has been turned into one of the best spots for live music in Rome. The surrounding area, with its lively squares and street music, is always buzzing. It is easy to find a good place for a drink or a bite to eat. From Thursdays to Sundays, Alcazar offers a mix of soul, funk, and jazz jams, alongside excellent cocktails, tasty food, and a retro atmosphere. You're guaranteed a memorable night out with a great crowd.

Via Cardinale Merry del Val, 14, 00153 Trastevere, alcazarlive.it

Vinille

In the trendy Ostiense district, you'll find the nightclub Vinile. With an old-school vibe, it's not overly fancy or full of exclusive frills. High ceilings, a spacious setting, and a slightly older crowd create a relaxed atmosphere, where you can enjoy an *aperitivo* followed by a great dinner. The evening starts with live music, and a DJ keeps the tunes going well into the night. Reservations can be made through the website.

Via Giuseppe Libetta, 19, 00154 Ostiense, vinileroma.it

La Conventicola Degli Ultramoderni

For something completely different, head to San Lorenzo, Rome's student neighbourhood near Termini station. It's full of street art, bars, and restaurants, plus La Conventicola Degli Ultramoderni. This burlesque club has an underground vaudeville vibe, offering experimental electronic music and a creative, unconventional atmosphere. This is truly unique and full of showmanship.

Via di Porta Labicana, 32, 00185 San Lorenzo, insta @conventicolaultramoderni

HOW TO DRESS LIKE A LOCAL

Dressing like a Roman no longer involves sandals, tunics or laurel wreaths. Modern-day Romans have their own uniform. They tend to dress a little on the formal side; you might call their style business casual. They're not as sharply dressed as the Milanese – the Roman's appearance is a bit more basic, in navy or grey. Thank heavens Romans keep their shirts properly buttoned to the top, though. Head further south in the boot, and you're not as lucky.

If you want to blend in, never dress as if you're heading to the beach when the temperatures rise. Don't even think about flip-flops. And don't look anything like you might be going to the gym either. Wet hair might also attract disapproving glances.

Romans, in general, dress according to the calendar. By September, summer is over, regardless of the temperature, and the summer wardrobe is tucked away. A navy quilted jacket is a must-have for Romans – after all, the *colpo d'aria* is always lurking around the corner; there might be a draft, and who knows what you might catch? And if the weather forecast hints at the slightest chance of rain, expect to see Romans clutching an umbrella all day long, just in case.

SECOND-HAND & VINTAGE

Ciao Vintage

Via del Governo Vecchio, 71, Centro Storico, insta @ciaovintage

A hotspot for thirty years now, Ciao Vintage is a treasure trove for vintage lovers looking for the big luxury brands. Timeless classics, bold prints, leather jackets you'll want to wear forever, accessories and jewellery with that Italian flair. Follow their Insta to stay updated on the latest arrivals and pop-up events.

Omero & Cecilia

Via del Governo Vecchio, 110, Centro Storico

A bit further down the same street, Omero & Cecilia is packed with a fascinating and wildly diverse collection of vintage pieces that somehow still all go together. Roll up your sleeves and start digging – you'll find items you never even knew you needed.

Cinzia

Via del Governo Vecchio, 45, Centro Storico, insta @vestiti_usati_cinzia

Cross the street and you'll find a third vintage paradise. Cinzia has been around since 1980 and specialises in fashion from the 60s, 70s, and 80s. As if time stood still, you'll easily spend a good amount of time at the shop, and you never know what you'll end up with – it could be anything from a baseball jacket to a quirky printed T-shirt or an evening gown.

SECOND-HAND & VINTAGE

Latini 34

*Via dei Sabelli, 36/38,
Centro Storico,
latini34.com*

Latini 34 merges vintage and contemporary styles, offering everything from retro bags to minimalist modern jewellery near Campo de' Fiori. This carefully curated boutique is driven by a passion for quality and authenticity. Each piece is hand-selected for its craftsmanship and history, blending designer finds with timeless classics while embracing sustainability.

Pifebo

*Via dei Serpenti, 135/136,
Monti; Via dei Valeri, 10,
San Giovanni,
insta @pifeboshop*

Effortlessly cool, Pifebo is a must-visit for vintage enthusiasts who are into the I'm-not-even-trying look. Both shops in Rome (one in Monti and one near the San Giovanni cathedral) offer an eclectic mix of more recent styles of leather goods, denim, and retro clothes. From jumpers and shirts that seem to come straight from your dad's wardrobe in the 90s, to tracksuit tops and T-shirts, boots, and sunglasses – the options are endless.

Humana Vintage

humanavintage.it

Part of a chain supporting sustainable fashion with shops in Milan, Bologna, and Rome, Humana Vintage offers pre-loved clothes with a funky twist. Their collection ranges from chic retro dresses to classic denim and unique statement pieces. Proceeds support charitable causes, making every purchase a feel-good investment.

Mercat Roma

Via di S. Francesco a Ripa, 25, Trastevere, merkat-roma.com

Mercat Roma is a trendy market blending vintage and contemporary styles in the heart of Rome. Located in a stylish, modern setting, it's perfect if you're looking for one-of-a-kind pieces with a creative edge. The mix includes vintage clothes, accessories from bags to (sun)glasses, handmade jewellery, and contemporary crafts. Check their website for upcoming events, as they occasionally host pop-ups and themed markets.

Twice Vintage

Via di S. Francesco a Ripa, 7, Trastevere, twicevintage.com

This boutique offers a selection of vintage and upcycled pieces. The shop features unique items from the 1920s to the 1990s, carefully curated with great attention to detail. Expect well-known brands, special accessories, bags, ties, jackets, and eyewear – all in excellent condition.

Sant'Egidio

Largo Fumasoni Biondi 5, 00153 Trastevere, insta @mercatoecosolidale

Sant'Egidio is what you may call the Roman version of the Salvation Army with a large network that collects and distributes of all sorts of used items and clothes. Many are donated but they also sell some to fund their projects. Sant'Egidio is run by volunteers. There's the (large!) Sant'Egidio Vintage Market in Ostiense and a tiny shop selling more high-end items in Trastevere. Both are open Friday to Sunday.

Porta Portese

Via Ettore Rolli, Trastevere

The legendary Porta Portese is the largest and most famous flea market in Rome, sprawling across Trastevere every Sunday morning. It's a chaotic paradise where you can find everything from vintage clothes and antiques to quirky knick-knacks and vinyl records. Arrive early to beat the crowds and bring cash as most vendors don't accept cards. Bargaining is expected, so don't hesitate to haggle a bit. While some stalls offer treasures, others lean towards mass-produced goods, so be ready to separate the wheat from the chaff to find great items. The atmosphere alone – lively, bustling, and quintessentially Roman – is worth the visit.

SiTenne

Via Cairoli, 55, 00185, Esquilino, insta @sitenne

This creative shop specialises in high-quality vintage fashion and unique accessories. Offering items from the 1920s to the 1990s, SiTenne caters to both fashion lovers and professionals, providing rental options for photographers, stylists, and filmmakers. If you happen to be going to a themed party while in Rome ... you'll know where to find your outfit!

Afare Fatto

Viale Aventino, 62, 00153 San Saba, affarefattomercatino.com

This shop is located near the FAO offices, and many parting diplomats have left behind a thing or two. The selection is incredibly varied in type, price, and quality, ranging from clothes to home accessories and furniture. With a bit of luck (and patience), you might uncover some real gems.

Mercatino Garbatella

Via Manfredo Camperio, 25, 00154 Garbatella, romagarbatella. mercatinousato.com

The Mercatino is Rome's equivalent of a charity shop chain, with multiple locations across the city. From furniture and home décor to clothes and books, it's an excellent spot for bargain hunters. The Mercatino in Garbatella is a neighbourhood favourite. Known for its friendly atmosphere and eclectic mix of items, it's perfect for those who enjoy leisurely browsing through second-hand finds.

Mademoiselle

Via Alberto da Giussano, 62e, 00176 Pigneto, mademoisellevintage.it

Step into Mademoiselle for a touch of Parisian charm. This boutique specialises in feminine vintage fashion, offering elegant dresses, chic accessories, and timeless classics. You can also book appointments for personal styling advice or a colour consultation. Once you know just what suits you best, discover the carefully selected pieces, from vintage and second-hand to handmade.

Mercatino Borghetto Flaminio

Piazza della Marina, 32, 00196 Flaminio, insta @borghetto_flaminio

This charming Sunday market near Piazza del Popolo is a favourite among locals and vintage enthusiasts. It is like raiding your very fashionable grandmother's wardrobe and it has a carefully selected range of second-hand and vintage items, from designer bags to unique jewellery and retro clothes. Prices can be higher than at Porta Portese, but the quality and uniqueness make it worth it. The crowd is often more upscale, the stalls are quite well-organised, and the vibe is relaxed, making it an enjoyable browsing experience.

STREETWEAR

One Block Down

Via Margutta 119, 00187 Centro Storico, oneblockdown.com

Adding to the many footsteps that have wandered Via Margutta, One Block Down adds a contemporary urban touch. It is a streetwear institution in Rome, offering a mix of international brands and exclusive collaborations. From limited-edition trainers to graphic tees and hoodies, this shop caters to serious sneakerheads and urban fashionistas.

Space 23

Corso Vittorio Emanuele II, 156, 00186 Centro Storico, space23.it

A small but notable chain with shops in Rome, Turin, Perugia and Bologna. The Space 23 shop at Corso Vittorio Emanuelle exudes fun, but the collection is no joke. *Tutte le sneakers che vuoi* – they carry all relevant brands in a carefully curated, head-to-toe collection.

Black Box

Via del Gambero, 7a, 00187 Centro Storico, blackboxstore.com

Just off Piazza di San Silvestro, Black Box carries a beautiful but not overwhelmingly large collection of trainers. With helpful and knowledgeable staff, you'll be out and on your way to the Spanish Steps in no time.

SUEDE Store

Via Cavour, 186, 00184 Monti, suede-store.com

When miles of sightseeing around Rome have worn you out, SUEDE, conveniently located at Via Cavour, will pick you up. This is a haven for trainer enthusiasts and streetwear lovers, as they stock all relevant brands, blending sportswear with urban fashion.

Airness

Via Giovanni Amendola, 15, 00184 Eqsuilino, airdom.com

This shop brings together street culture and sportswear, offering trainers, hoodies, and other essentials from global and local brands. Airness is a great spot for those who want a sporty edge to their street style.

FASHION & DEPARTMENT STORES

Atelier Bomba

Via dell'Oca, 39, 00186 Centro Storico, insta @ atelierbomba

Founded in 1980, Atelier Bomba is a family-run atelier specialising in demi-couture. Located near Piazza del Popolo, it offers handcrafted tailoring with vintage and high-quality fabrics. Every piece is individually cut and sewn by skilled artisans, ensuring refinement, sustainability, and timeless elegance.

La Rinascente

Via del Tritone, 61, 00187 Centro Storico, rinascente.it

La Rinascente is a high-end department store that you can find in some major Italian cities. It offers luxury fashion, beauty products, homeware, gourmet food, and designer accessories. The Rinascente flagship store at Via del Tritone has a rooftop terrace with a view. In the basement, you can see a fully functioning ancient aqueduct!

Martha Ray

Via dei Coronari, 150, 00186 Centro Storico, martaray.it

Martha Ray is focused on sustainability, offering a collection of chic and timeless shoes, bags, and accessories. Each piece is designed to blend style with eco-consciousness. Many items are available in multiple colours, giving you a perfect range to choose from.

Hang Roma

Via degli Zingari, 32, 00184 Monti, hangroma.it

Hang Roma creates handcrafted bags inspired by architecture and urban life. Made in Italy, their designs adapt to different needs — think backpacks that transform into shoulder bags. Using high-quality materials, they blend craftsmanship with contemporary, functional design that is not aimed at a single gender.

Coloriage

Via della Lungaretta, 16, 00153 Trastevere, coloriage.it

Coloriage is a social tailoring workshop and free fashion school in Trastevere. It serves as a creative meeting space where designers and artisans from different backgrounds share skills and techniques to craft unique pieces. At Coloriage, reclaimed fabrics from Italian deadstock are combined with handcrafted textiles and batik from West Africa, reflecting a blend of traditions.

Coin Excelsior

Via Cola di Rienzo, 173 Prati, coin.it

Coin Excelsior is a modern department store. It offers a selection of high-end fashion, beauty products, and home goods, featuring both Italian and international brands. The store has a contemporary design and a well-curated selection.

BOOKSHOPS

Otherwise

Via del Governo Vecchio, 80, 00186 Centro Storico, otherwisebookshop.it

A modern independent bookshop with a strong focus on English-language books. Otherwise offers a selection of fiction, non-fiction, and children's books. A beautiful choice of books about Rome makes it the perfect spot to get a literary souvenir. They also host literary events and author readings.

Altroquando

Via del Governo Vecchio, 82, 00186 Centro Storico, altroquando.com

Opposite its sister Otherwise, Altroquando isn't just another bookshop. It's a cultural hub with a small bar where visitors can sip their drink while perusing its unique selection. They specialise in independent publications, graphic novels, and art books. With its artistic vibe, Altroquando is a place that invites you to linger. Below, you'll find underground pub Anderquando. An alternative, relaxed space for those who love a bit of eclectic energy with their drink.

Booktique

Via della Stelletta 17, 00186 / Via degli Orfani 80, 00186 Centro Storico, Roma, booktique.info

Booktique is a charming independent bookshop and cabinet of stylish curiosities that offers carefully curated books across various genres and Rome-themed items that you would actually want to take home. A *Mai'na gioa* shopper, anyone?

Feltrinelli

multiple locations, including Largo di Torre Argentina, 5, 00186 Centro Storico, lafeltrinelli.it

Feltrinelli is one of Italy's largest bookstore chains, and its Rome locations offer a reliable selection of books in various languages. If you are after a quick purchase or a specific title, this is a convenient option. Some branches also have cafés, allowing visitors to relax while reading.

Spazio Sette Libreria

Via dei Barbieri, 7, 00186 Centro Storico, spaziosette.ubiklibri.it

An elegant bookshop, housed in a beautiful historic building. Spazio Sette Libreria has a diverse collection of books, including art, design, and architecture publications. The space also serves as a cultural hub, hosting literary and artistic events. The refined atmosphere makes it a pleasant place to browse.

Libri Necessari

Via degli Zingari, 22, 00184 Monti, librinecessari.it

Libri Necessari is a small independent bookshop specialising in philosophy, literature, and niche publications. Its curated selection makes it an excellent place for those looking for rare or thought-provoking reads. The intimate setting adds to its charm.

Borri Books

Stazione Termini, 00185 Esquilino, borribooks.com

Located inside Termini Station, Borri Books is a three-storey bookshop with a wide selection in multiple languages. It is a convenient option for travellers looking to pick up a book before their journey. Borri offers everything from bestsellers to classics and travel guides.

Almost Corner Bookshop

Via del Moro, 45, Trastevere, insta @almostcornerbookshop

This small but well-stocked bookshop in Trastevere is a favourite among English-speaking visitors as well as locals. They have a wide selection of English-language books, including fiction, travel guides, and historical texts. The knowledgeable staff offer excellent recommendations.

Open Door Bookshop

Via della Lunguretta, 23, 00153 Trastevere, opendoorbookshop.it

Open Door Bookshop, in the heart of Trastevere, is a second-hand bookshop that specialises in English, French, and Italian books. It is an excellent place to find affordable reads, including classics, contemporary novels, and academic books. The relaxed and welcoming atmosphere makes it a great spot to explore.

Libreria Antigone

Via dei Piceni, 29, 00185 San Lorenzo, libreriantigone.com

Libreria Antigone is an LGBTQ+-focused bookshop that offers a diverse selection of books on gender, identity, and social issues. It is an important cultural space in Rome, promoting inclusivity and awareness through literature and community events.

ART SUPPLIES

Ditta G. Poggi

Via del Gesù, 74-75, 00186 Centro Storico, poggi1825.it

Ditta G. Poggi has been selling pigments, brushes, canvases, crayons, and anything else you might need for painting, drawing, and restoration since 1825. Founded by Gaspare Poggi as *Ditta delle belle arti*, this shop has served from fresco artists to portraitists, and artists of all kinds. Just steps from the Pantheon and Collegio Romano, it has always been a trusted supplier known for its expertise and wide selection.

Antica Cartotechnica

Piazza dei Caprettari, 61, 00186 Centro Storico, anticacartotecnica.it

This third-generation family-owned business between the Pantheon and Piazza Navona, has been open since 1930. With floor-to-ceiling vintage shelves filled with both old and new pens, leather notebooks, wallets, folders, and vintage items, this historic shop is ideal for those seeking distinctive paper goods, fountain pens, and traditional Italian craftsmanship.

Vertecchi

Via Vitorchiano,26, 00189 Centro Storico, shop.vertecchi.com

A well-established art supply shop offering a wide selection of professional materials. From high-quality paints, brushes, and canvases to notebooks, washi tape, and stationery, Vertecchi caters to both professional artists and hobbyists. With several branches in Rome, it is a go-to spot for creative supplies, offering a more accessible option for beginners compared to a more serious painter's shop.

↓ ANTICA CARTOTECHNICA

AFFORDABLE ART & HOME DECO

Mercato delle Stampe

Piazza Borghese, 00186 Centro Storico

Located in Piazza Borghese, Mercato delle Stampe is a historical open-air market specialising in vintage prints, antique books, and rare illustrations. It is the perfect place to find unique posters and decorative artwork at reasonable prices. The variety of prints available ensures that there is something for every taste and style.

Fox Gallery

Corso Vittorio Emanuele II, 5, 00186 Centro Storico, fox-gallery.scontrinoshop.com

Fox Gallery is a contemporary art space that features a mix of paintings, fantastic prints, and small design objects. This gallery supports local artists, making it a great place to discover affordable artwork. Visitors can find beautifully crafted posters, decorative ceramics, and stylish home accessories.

Museo del Louvre

Via della Reginella, 00186 Centro Storico, ilmuseodellouvre.com

A boutique-style shop offering high-quality prints, handmade paper products, and vintage-inspired home décor. The range at Museo del Louvre includes posters, some 30,000 vintage photos, coffee table books, and artisanal home accessories that come together in a delightfully quirky atmosphere.

Flakes Design

Via della Scala, 45, Trastevere, shop. flakesarredo.com

A stop at Flakes Design in Trastevere is a must – after all, you'll want a vintage plate saying *Ho Ancora Fame* after your trip to Rome. You'll find a selection of hand-crafted ceramic pieces from all over Italy with a focus on sustainability. Its stylish and colourful selection has an appreciation of traditional statement pieces.

VINYL & CDS

Vino e Vinilli

*Via del Pellegrino, 77
00186 Centro Storico,
insta @vinoevinilliroma*

Vino e Vinilli in Centro Storico combines a passion for vinyl with a love of wine, which makes it an inviting space. Here you can enjoy a nice glass of wine, carefully selected from wineries across Italy, while listening to and browsing through the vinyl collection with records from the 70s and 80s.

Soul Food

Via San Giovanni in Laterano 192/194, 00184 Monti, haterecords.com

Situated between the Colosseum and San Giovanni cathedral, Soul Food is a record shop dedicated to soul, funk, jazz, and rare grooves. The shop has a strong focus on vinyl, with an excellent collection that appeals to both serious collectors and casual listeners. It's well-known for its knowledgeable staff, who are always ready to offer recommendations.

Welcome to the Jungle

Via Monte Zebio, 44A, 00195 Prati, wttjrecordstore.it

Named after the famous Guns N' Roses song, Welcome to the Jungle is an indie record shop that also hosts live events, making it a key part of the local music scene. Specialising in rock music in the broadest sense, it boasts an impressive selection of vinyl, from rare finds to recent releases, and is a popular spot for both collectors and music lovers.

Radiation Records

radiationrecords.net

Radiation Records is a small chain of three shops in Pigneto, Monti and Trastevere. They sell both new and used vinyl, along with CDs, books, gadgets, and T-shirts. Specialising in second-hand vinyl, they import hundreds of used records each week. Radiation Records also reissues vinyl under their own label, Radiation Reissues.

SHOPS WE LOVE

Laura

Via di Campo Marzio 35 / Via dei Coronari, 57, 00186 Centro Storico, essenzialmentelaura.it

Laura is a fragrance boutique specialising in unique, high-quality perfumes crafted by renowned perfumer Laura Bosetti Tonatto. Known internationally as a 'nose', she has been creating bespoke scents and working with major cosmetic companies since 1986. With expertise that extends to academia — she teaches the art of perfumery and aromacology at the University of Ferrara — her boutique offers an exquisite selection of locally crafted fragrances.

Co.Ro

Via della Scrofa, 62, 00186 Centro Storico, corojewels.com

A collaboration between local jewellers, Co.Ro creates wearable statement pieces inspired by Italy's monuments and architecture. The collections combine elegance with modern design, offering unique, bold, and stylish souvenirs. Drawing inspiration from Baroque splendour to industrial architecture, Co.Ro blends modern design with traditional craftsmanship.

Giuncart

Via del Pellegrino, 77, 00186 Centro Storico, insta @giuncart

Giuncart is a charming, family-owned boutique, filled floor-to-ceiling with beautifully crafted wicker baskets, straw bags, and other woven goods. Recognisable by the Piaggio Ape outside, this shop is where you go for locally made pieces that do not scream souvenir.

Il Marmoraro

Via Margutta, 53B, 00187 Centro Storico, insta @bottegadelmarmoraro

Via Margutta has always been a street of artisans, and the *bottega* of Il Marmoraro is the last one of its kind. A visit to this unique mini museum, workshop, and shop is a lesson in Roman proverbs and sayings. You might hear a fascinating anecdote from Sandro, the *marmoraro* himself. This shop specialises in handcrafted marble plaques and decorative objects, making it the perfect place to find a meaningful and authentic souvenir.

PARKS AND SWIMMING

Villa Borghese

Villa Borghese is probably Rome's most famous park. It is located north of the Spanish Steps, with views of Piazza del Popolo from the Pincio Hill. Originally designed as a garden for the Borghese family in the 17th century, it combines natural beauty with cultural landmarks, including Galleria Borghese Museum and Museo Carlo Bilotti.

Villa Pamphilij

Villa Pamphilij, Rome's largest landscaped park, is west of the city centre in the Gianicolo district. The historic estate dates to the 17th century and was created as a country retreat for the Pamphilij family. It features expansive gardens, wooded areas, and walking trails, along with the grand Casino del Bel Respiro (in use by the government). If you have the time, take tram 8 to Casaletto, enter the park from Via Leone XII, enjoy the view and walk back downhill.

Villa Celimontana

Located on the Caelian Hill near the Colosseum, Villa Celimontana is a smaller, quieter park with a rich history. The villa's grounds include gardens, romantic 'Roman' remains, and an obelisk from Egypt. Today, it is a peaceful space, where occasionally outdoor events and concerts take place.

Villa Torlonia

Villa Torlonia, located on Via Nomentana, was the 19th-century estate of the Torlonia

family. The neoclassical villa is surrounded by picturesque gardens and features unique structures like the whimsical Casina delle Civette, 'House of the Owls'. The site, once used as Mussolini's residence, is now a public park with museums in the villa's buildings.

Parco Caffarella

Part of the larger Appian Way Regional Park, Parco Caffarella is a vast green space filled with history and nature. The park features ancient ruins, including the Ninfeo Egeria and the Tomb of Annia Regilla, alongside open fields, shaded trails, a medieval tower, and a small stream. Popular with joggers, cyclists, and families, it offers a peaceful escape while still being close to the historic centre.

Villa Sciarra

On the slopes of the Gianicolo, Villa Sciarra is a charming, lesser-known park offering shaded walkways, fountains, and beautifully sculpted gardens. Once a private estate, it is now a public park with a serene atmosphere, perfect for a quiet stroll. The park is adorned with statues and mythological figures, creating a unique blend of nature and art.

Parco degli Acquedotti

Situated near the ancient Roman Via Appia, the Parco degli Acquedotti is named after the magnificent Aqua Claudia, Aqua Felice, and Aqua Marcia aqueducts that run through it. The park is a popular spot to go for a run or have a picnic. It is easily accessible from the Giulio Agricola metro station and offers a remarkable spot to catch a glimpse of Rome's ancient engineering marvels.

Piscina Le Mura

In the hot summer months, when you can't decide between admiring ancient monuments

and taking a refreshing dip, you don't have to. Piscina Le Mura is a public pool with a spectacular view of the ancient aqueducts. The pool is located centrally in the Furio Camillo area (metro A, Furio Camillo).

Via Piegaro, 174, 00181 Tuscolano

Lago di Bracciano

Lago di Bracciano, located just outside Rome, is a large volcanic lake known for its crystal-clear waters. It's a popular spot for swimming, sailing, and other outdoor activities. The area is also home to charming lakeside villages, perfect for a relaxing day trip from the city. You can reach Bracciano by train from Stazione di San Pietro.

Piscina delle Rose

If you're serious about swimming in Rome, take metro B to the strictly neoclassical 1930s district of EUR. The Piscina delle Rose, built for the 1960 Olympics, dates to the *Dolce Vita* years. You can swim your laps here, but there's also plenty of space to sunbathe. It's open daily from 9am to 7pm, with weekday admission of 10 euros. On weekends, they charge double, but half-day rates are also available.

Viale America 20, Passeggiata del Giappone, snc, 00144, EUR, piscinadellerose.com

VEGETARIAN AND VEGAN ROME

Given the cuisine's emphasis on cheese and meat, vegetarians and vegans might have hesitations about the Roman food scene. But even the more traditional venues always have enough options, as there are a variety of dishes that are naturally vegetarian or easily adapted for vegan diets. *Carciofi alla Romana* are artichokes braised with garlic, mint, and parsley, creating a tender and flavourful dish. *Pasta e ceci* is a hearty pasta and chickpea soup, often seasoned with rosemary and garlic. *Fiori di zucca*, or stuffed zucchini flowers, are typically filled with cheese and fried but can be made vegan with alternatives such as cashew-based fillings. *Puntarelle* is a crisp dish made from chicory shoots, dressed with garlic, olive oil, and traditionally anchovy, which can be omitted or replaced. *Cicoria ripassata* consists of sautéed chicory greens with garlic and chili, offering a slightly bitter and spicy side dish. There are also plenty of plant-based restaurants. Here are some good suggestions.

Ginger Sapori e Saluti

Craving something green and healthy? Ginger, with three locations in the city centre (all in Centro Storico), is never far away. Their fresh juices are a must for anyone in need of a healthy break. Ginger focuses on health-conscious dining, emphasising fresh, organic, and sustainable ingredients. Dishes range from gourmet paninis to pasta dishes and very generous salads to fresh fruit smoothies.

gingersaporiesalute.com

Ecru

Ecru specialises in raw, organic, and vegan dishes, maintaining a cruelty-free and zero food miles policy. Their menu features a variety of plant-based options, including raw desserts and cold-pressed juices. Their spin on the Waldorf salad is the perfect lunch dish. The ambience is modern but warm and all their artwork is for sale.

Via Acciaioli, 13, 00186 Centro Storico, ecrurawfood.it

Aromaticus

With locations in Monti and Trastevere, Aromaticus is a refuge for plant enthusiasts and foodies alike. It is a fresh and colourful bistro, with a menu full of tasty vegetarian and vegan options. Dishes are prepared using fresh, organic ingredients, reflecting a philosophy of healthy and sustainable eating. The eatery's calm atmosphere makes it an ideal spot to unwind for a bit before you head out for more sightseeing.

Via Urbana, 134, 00184 Centro Storico / Via Natale del Grande, 6/7, 00153 Trastevere aromaticus-roma.com

Il Margutta

Established in 1979, Il Margutta was Italy's first vegetarian restaurant. Located on Via Margutta, it serves a sophisticated menu that changes with the seasons, ensuring the freshest ingredients are used. Their brunches are particularly popular, offering a wide array of vegetarian and vegan dishes in a buffet setting. The restaurant doubles as an art gallery.

Via Margutta, 118, 00187 Centro Storico, ilmargutta.bio

Rifugio Romano

It's almost like making the impossible possible – a vegan version of Roman cuisine. But Rifugio Romano does just that. Situated near Termini Station, you can enjoy plant-based adaptations of traditional Roman and Italian dishes in a laid-back atmosphere.

Via Volturno, 39/41, 00185 Castro Pretorio, rifugioromano.com

100% BIO

Opposite the Porta San Paolo, 100% BIO provides a buffet of organic, vegan, and vegetarian dishes. If you'd like to enjoy a healthy breakfast, lunch, *aperitivo* or dinner in a relaxed and friendly setting, with a side of ancient architecture, this is where to go.

Piazza di Porta S. Paolo, 6/a, 00153 San Saba/Ostiense, centopercento.bio

Vegan Store Mercato Testaccio

Within Mercato Testaccio, the Vegan Store stands out by offering a wide selection of plant-based products, from vegan cheeses to vegan meat alternatives, snacks, and other speciality items.

Via Aldo Manuzio, 66b, 00153 Testaccio, mercatoditestaccio.it/banco/vegan-store

Col Cavolo

Col Cavolo is a vegan bistro in the Trieste neighbourhood, known for its creative plant-based dishes and impressive vegan spin on the classics. *Lasagna* as a main and *tiramisù* for dessert, anyone? The menu is crafted with a focus on flavour and sustainability. The inviting interior and friendly staff make it a local favourite.

Via Cesare Bosi, 7, 00198 Salario, insta @colcavoloveganbistrot

Ops!

For an elaborate, fresh vegan buffet-style lunch or dinner in Rome, make your way to Via Bergamo, in the trendy Salario neighbourhood, just outside Porta Pia. Ops! is a popular vegan restaurant that offers a variety of plant-based dishes, fresh salads, pasta, and creative mains that is charged by weight.

Via Bergamo, 56, 00198 Salario, opsveg.com

OUTSIDE OF ROME

Ostia Antica

Parco Archeologico di Ostia Antica, Viale dei Romagnoli, 717, 00119, Roma, ostiaantica. beniculturali.it

A short 25-minute metro ride from Roma-Ostiense/Porta S. Paulo takes you to Ostia Antica, Rome's well-preserved ancient harbour town, offering a fascinating glimpse into everyday life during the times of the Roman Republic and Empire. Once the bustling port of ancient Rome, Ostia was a crucial hub for trade, connecting the city to the Mediterranean and beyond. Today, the expansive ruins offer an impressive insight into life in the Roman Empire. The remains of grand bathhouses, temples, mosaics, and the ancient theatre that once hosted performances for thousands of spectators, are quite spectacular. Ostia Antica is usually far less crowded than other similar sites (like Pompeii) and wandering through the ancient, well-preserved streets is worth the visit.

Castelli Romani

The Castelli Romani is a group of picturesque, charming medieval towns nestled in the Alban Hills, about twenty kilometres southeast of Rome. The region is famous for its volcanic lakes, rolling hills, and beautiful vineyards. The area's most notable towns include Frascati,

Castel Gandolfo, Ariccia, and Albano Laziale. These towns were popular summer retreats for ancient Roman aristocrats. They have not lost their appeal, with their historic architecture, delicious local wines, and scenic landscapes.

Castel Gandolfo

Castel Gandolfo overlooks Lake Albano, a volcanic crater lake, and offers breathtaking views of its surroundings. The Pope's residence, the Apostolic Palace, was used as a shelter for all town residents during WWII. The beautiful gardens were designed by the renowned Renaissance architect Carlo Maderno. The town itself is also worth a visit. Trains from Roma Termini to Castel Gandolfo run about once an hour.

Frascati

Known for its historic villas and wine, Frascati is a popular day trip from Rome. Frascati has been a favourite getaway for centuries, dating back to ancient Roman times. One of the most beautiful villas of the town, Villa Aldobrandini, is still owned by the same family. It boasts impressive Baroque gardens. Frascati is also renowned for its wine, especially its white wine, with many vineyards offering tours and tastings. Trains from Roma Termini to Frascati run about once an hour.

TO THE BEACH

Rome may not be a coastal city, but its proximity to the Tyrrhenian Sea makes a beach escape a breeze. Several seaside towns are within an hour's reach.

Santa Marinella

Train station:
Stazione S. Marinella

One of the most convenient beach destinations, Santa Marinella is located about 60 km northwest of Rome. It's easily accessible by train from Termini, Ostiense, Trastevere and San Pietro stations, with the journey taking around 45 minutes. The town features a long stretch of sandy shoreline and a relaxed vibe. There aren't many free beach areas, but sunbeds (and parasols!) are available at the beach clubs.

Santa Severa

Stationsweg 94, 3151 HS
Hoek van Holland

Santa Severa, about 44 kilometres northwest of Rome, is a scenic beach adorned by a historic castle right by the shore. The train ride from Roma Termini takes just under an hour, making it an easy day trip. While some *spiaggia libera* exist, most visitors opt for private *stabilimenti* with sunbeds and parasols for rent. The relaxed atmosphere and striking coastal views make it a favourite escape from the city.

Fregene

A bit more complicated to reach by public transport (a train ride plus a bus or taxi), but about an hour by car, Fregene lies west of Rome and is a favourite among locals. Known for its lively beach clubs, Fregene attracts a younger crowd, especially on weekends.

Antica Monterano

Str. Antica Monterano, 00060 Canale Monterano, monteranoriserva.it

Antica Monterano is an atmospheric, abandoned town in the Lazio region, about sixty kilometres northwest of Rome. Perched on a tuff hill near Canale Monterano, it offers striking ruins, including the remains of a Baroque church and a ducal palace (with a façade designed by Bernini), an aqueduct, and a grand fountain featuring a lion sculpture. The town was abandoned in the late 18th century, after malaria outbreaks and conflicts drove its residents away. Today, it's a popular spot for hikers and history enthusiasts. You can reach Antica Monterano by car in about two hours.

INDEX

Neighbourhoods 8
Practical info 12
Travel 14
Where to stay 20
Good to know 24
When to travel 30
Life in Rome 40
History 42
Sightseeing 52
Museums 60
Street art 68
Cinema 72
Festivals 74
Things to do 78
Famous people 82
Films & series in and about Rome 86
Books in & about Rome 90
Fun facts 96
Photo spots 100
Food and drinks 106
Going out 130
Shopping 142
Green Rome 170
Parks and swimming 172
Vegetarian and vegan Rome 179
Outside of Rome 184
To the beach 186

GOING OUT 130
Al Vino Al Vino 133
Alcazar Live 138
Antica Birreria Perroni 132
Bar dei Brutti 137
Bar San Calisto 136
Bars 136
Beer 132
Clubs 138
Coming Out Roma 137
Conventicola Degli Ultramoderni, La 139
Enoteca Buccone 133

Freni e Frizioni 137
Goccetto, Il 133
Jungle Juice 132
Ma Che Siete Venuti a Fà 132
My Bar 138
Piccolo, Il 132
Queer 137
Samovar 137
Sanctuary, The 138
Sharivari 138
Tartarughe 136
Vinille 139
Wine 132

FOOD & DRINKS 106
200 Gradi 113
Antico caffè Grecco 109
Aperitivo 121
Bar Farnese 108
Bibliobar 123
Borgosteria 112
Breakfast 108
Bring the parents 128
Buvette, La 122
Camillo dal 1890 121
Casa Manfredi 109
Castroni 119
Civico 4 123
Dar Ciriola 113
Dinner 124
Eataly 119
Faro – Caffè Specialty 110
Felice a Testaccio 127
Forno Conti 109
Forno Roscioli 113
Gelateria del Teatro 121
Gelato 121
Giulio Passami l'Olio 124
Libera Soon 110
Licata, La 109

Lunch 110
Maccheroni 112
Marchese, Il 124
Markets 116
Mercaot Campagna Amica al Circo Massimo 119
Mercato Plesbiscito 108
Mercato Rionale Monti 116
Mercato Testaccio 116
Mercato Trionfale 116
Necci dal 1924 113
Oro Bistrot 129
Osteria delle Copelle 124
Pasticceria Andreotti dal1931 110
Pasticceria Linari 110
Pianostrada 124
Pierluigi 128
Pizza 123
Pizza al taglio 114
Ristorante Brocoletti 126
Ristorante Piperno 128
Rocco 126
Salotto 42 122
Shops (food) 119
Six Senses Rome 129
Street food 114
Supplizio 114
Tazzo d'Oro & Sant'Eustacchio 108
Terrazza Borromini 129
Tiberino 112
Tram Depot 123
Trapizzino 114
Trattoria Da Enzo al 29 127
Trattoria de Gli Amici, La 127
Trattoria Pennestri 127
Zanzara, La 113
Zia Rosetta 112

MUSEUMS 60
Capitoline Museums 60
Castel Sant'Angelo 66
Centrale Montemartini 66
Chiostro del Bramante 62
Galleria Borghese 63
Galleria Corsini 64
Galleria Doria Pamphilj 61
Galleria Spada 62
MAXXI 67
Mercati di Traiano 60
Museo della Forma Urbis 62
Palazzo Colonna 60
Palazzo Massimo alle Terme 63
Vatican Museums 64
Villa Farnesina 64

PHOTO SPOTS 100
Giardinetto del Monte Oppio 100
Palazzo Braschi 103
Pantheon 103
Piazza del Popolo 100
Ponte Umberto I 100
Santa Maria Maggiore 104
Trajan's Column 104
Trastevere 104
Via del Campidoglio 103
Via Margutta 104

SHOPPING 142
How to dress like a local 144
Affordable art & home deco 164
Art supplies 162
Shops we love 168
Vinyl & cds 167

Bookshops 158
Almost Corner Bookshop 160
Altroquando 158
Booktique 158
Borri Books 159
Feltrinelli 159
Libreria Antigone 160
Libri Necessari 159
Open Door Bookshop
Otherwise 158
Spazio Sette Libreria 159

Fashion & department stores 154
Atelier Bomba 154
Coin Excelsior 155
Coloriage 155

Hang Roma 155
Martha Ray 154
Rinascente, La 154

Second-hand & vintage 146
Afare Fatto 150
Ciao Vintage 146
Cinzia 146
Humana Vintage 148
Latini 34 148
Mademoiselle 151
Mercat Roma 149
Mercatino Borghetto 151
Mercatino Garbatella 151
Omero & Cecilia 146
Pifebo 148
Porta Portese 150
Sant'Egidio 149
SiTenne 150
Twice Vintage 149

Streetwear 152
Airness 153
Black Box 153
One Block Down 153
Space 23 153
SUEDE Store 153

SIGHTSEEING 52
Chiesa del Gesù & Sant'Ignazio di Loyala 56
Piazza del Campidoglio 52
Piazza del Popolo 57
Piazza Mattei 53
Quartieere Coppeè 58
Santa Maria della Pace & San Luigi dei Francesci 56
Santa Prassede 57
Trevi Fountain 57

Vegetarian & vegan Rome 179
100% BIO 182
Aromaticus 181
Col Cavolo 182
Ecru 181
Ginger Sapori e Saluti 179
Margutta, Il 181
Ops! 182
Rifugio Romano 181
Vegan Store Mercato Testaccio 182

ABOUT THE AUTHOR

Non basta una vita! – A lifetime is not enough. That's what a friend's quintessentially Roman mother told Jessica at the start of her first trip to the city, many years ago. She had just asked if a week would be enough to see everything. As she was writing this guide, Jessica had just returned to Amsterdam after spending five unforgettable years in Rome. In the Eternal City, she combined her background in art history with her experience in education and cultural production. She worked with travel agents, production companies, and as a tourguide and travel writer. Having lived in several different neighbourhoods and possessing endless curiosity, she explored the city thoroughly, each time struck by its beauty. The Roman *mamma* had been right: there's always more left to discover.

WHY SHOULD I GO TO ROME
the city you definitely need to visit
before you turn 30 (or 130)

Published in 2025 by
mo'media Rotterdam,
The Netherlands, momedia.nl

Concept
mo'media

Text and address selection
Jessica Schots

Art direction and illustration design
Jelle F. Post

Editing
Ezra van Wilgenburg, Maaike van Steekelenburg

Photography
Vincent van den Hoogen e.a.

All rights reserved. No part of this publication may be copied, displayed, extracted, reproduced, utilised, stored in a retrieval system or transmitted in any form or by any means, electronic, mechanical or otherwise including but not limited to photocopying, recording, or scanning without the prior written permission of the publisher.

 Copyright © mo'media BV, 2025

Why Should I Go To Rome
ISBN 978 94 9333 869 2
NUR 510

Disclaimer
The points of interested mentioned in this travel guide have been selected by the author. None of them have been paid for inclusion in this book: the *Why Should I Go To* book series is entirely ad-free.

Publisher's Note
Every effort has been made to ensure that the information in this book is accurate at the time of going to press. The publisher welcomes any information or suggestions for correction or improvement. Please send us an e-mail at info@momedia.nl.

 whyshouldigoto

WHY SHOULD I GO TO?
Information on all our travel guides
on **WHYSHOULDIGOTO.COM**

Why Should I Go To travel guides are available for the following cities: Amsterdam, Antwerp, Barcelona, Berlin, Budapest, Copenhagen, London, Paris, Prague, Valencia, and Rotterdam. More cities will be added soon.